MORE SIMPLE CAFÉ FOOD

PENGUIN
BOOKS

MORE SIMPLE
CAFÉ FOOD

Julie Le Clerc

Photography by Shaun Cato-Symonds

Penguin Books

PENGUIN BOOKS

Penguin Books (NZ) Ltd, cnr Airborne and Rosedale Roads, Albany,
Auckland 1310, New Zealand
Penguin Books Ltd, 27 Wrights Lane, London W8 5TZ, England
Penguin Putnam Inc, 375 Hudson Street, New York, NY 10014, United States
Penguin Books Australia Ltd, 487 Maroondah Highway, Ringwood, Australia 3134
Penguin Books Canada Ltd, 10 Alcorn Avenue, Toronto, Ontario, Canada M4V 3B2
Penguin Books (South Africa) Pty Ltd, 5 Watkins Street,
Denver Ext 4, 2094, South Africa
Penguin Books India (P) Ltd, 11, Community Centre, Panchsheel Park,
New Delhi 110 017, India

Penguin Books Ltd, Registered Offices: Harmondsworth, Middlesex, England

First published by Penguin Books (NZ) Ltd, 2000
1 3 5 7 9 10 8 6 4 2
Copyright © text, Julie Le Clerc, 2000
Copyright © photographs, Shaun Cato-Symonds, 2000

The right of Julie Le Clerc to be identified as the author of this work in terms of section 96 of the
Copyright Act 1994 is hereby asserted.

Designed and typeset by Seven
Printed by Condor Production, Hong Kong

ISBN 0 14 029792 8

ACKNOWLEDGEMENTS

There are many people I wish to thank and I feel fortunate because producing a book like this gives me a wonderful opportunity to do so.

A big thank you has to go to my loyal (past and present) team at the Garnet Road Foodstore who have always been a magic, hard-working, fun-loving bunch and very important personalities in the café.

My most sincere thanks go to all my dedicated customers, many of whom have become good friends.

A special acknowledgement must be given to all who so enthusiastically bought, cooked from and enjoyed my first book, *Simple Café Food*.

Grateful thanks to my suppliers for providing such excellent raw materials, service, knowledge and advice.

My love and thanks go to my dear family and friends who understood when I disappeared into solitary concentration and were still there when I emerged much later with the book completed.

I am indebted to Shaun Cato-Symonds for such absolutely brilliant photography. I am continually overwhelmed by the beauty and splendour of your work and your commitment to perfectly capturing mine on film. I have very happy memories of the synchronous hours we spent together producing the pictures that so eloquently grace the pages of this book.

Many thanks to Penguin Books (NZ) for fostering this project, especially Bernice Beachman and Philippa Gerrard for your nurturing enthusiasm, lots of laughter and encouragement, and of course your solid work in production. Also Callum Hayes for your excellent promotional skills, chats over coffee and books, and a little MG.

Thank you Anne Russell for your gentle and skilful editing.

To Gideon Keith, for the book's stunning design, which has been greatly admired and appreciated.

Thanks to Rachel Carley once again for contributing to the pages of this book, not only your beautiful china but also this time your own porcelain features. You're a star.

And to Kevin Emirali, thanks for your excellent modelling assistance, fun didgeridoo lessons and company over lunch.

INTRODUCTION

I have been deeply rewarded by the phenomenal response to my first cookbook, *Simple Café Food*. I felt so encouraged that I enthusiastically wrote this book to give you 'more' of my café-style recipes that have proved so popular. Hundreds of people have given me overwhelming encouragement, touching praise and invaluable feedback about *Simple Café Food*. The overall comment is that they have felt inspired, and I could not ask for a more satisfying reaction to my efforts.

People tell me that they are all cooking from 'the book' and with great success. Others tell me of the innovations they have made to my recipes; this is the greatest compliment I could receive because they are using the book as I intended it to be used. We all gather ideas and influences that are in turn assimilated into the food we like to cook.

The thing about cooking is that it is eclectic and evolving. The type of food people naturally cook is like a statement about their life, where they've been, who has inspired them, what they like. I find it hard to explain why I love cooking so much. It is something that comes from deep inside me and goes way back. For me, one of the most exciting things about cooking is that it appeals so completely to all the senses and is therefore very satisfying to be fully immersed in. I feel fortunate to have cooking as my career and I approach it with a generous spirit, passionate hands and an enquiring mind.

The idea is to indulge your fancies. Both cooking and eating should give the greatest of pleasure. Use raw materials joyfully. Focus on ingredients and care about them and then everything will fall into place beautifully.

The main difference between cooking for a café and cooking at home lies in the preparation of ingredients or 'mise en place'. Many hours of teamwork are spent peeling, chopping and dicing to bring produce to a state of readiness for final assemblage and service in a café. The home cook can emulate this procedure on a smaller scale and indeed, employing such principles will make cooking at home more streamlined. Other differences lie in the quantity of food produced and professional experience or a sure feel for combining flavours and creating recipes.

This is where my book will be most useful because it contains recipes that are the result of years of refinement. The beauty of such refined recipes is that their simple execution makes them achievable no matter how limited or advanced your cooking skills. These are colourful, flavourful and yet simple dishes that stand the test of time. Remember that recipes are neither concrete nor even remotely permanent; most dishes continue to be reworked according to the whims of the person cooking, the availability of fresh produce or sometimes whatever is on hand in the fridge and the demands of eaters.

Café eating does not follow a formal entrée, main, dessert format and so neither do the chapters in this book. Café dwellers don't seem to follow any particular rules either. For example, and this may sound extraordinary, people will often have soup or even cake for breakfast. Coffee accompanies all courses. It's a mix and match kind of situation and that is how you can use this book. Some cakes will make a great breakfast item but could also be a dessert. Small food could be cooked in larger amounts and become a main meal. Add meat to a vegetarian dish or replace a meat with something like tofu if you prefer. Recipes are guidelines only, so let your imagination go wild.

Nearly all the ingredients in this book are readily available in supermarkets or the average kitchen cupboard. If I have included the odd thing that may be harder to find I have suggested substitutions that will work perfectly well. One of the joys of cooking to me is experimenting with new flavours and ingredients, so hunt these out with enthusiasm if you can. By creating a demand, we the customers can only benefit.

I present with this book 'more' simple café food and a nostalgic embrace of my time in the café kitchen. The recipes evoke some of the ambience of café life; through the pages of this book you can soak up the smells, hear the laughter, meet some of the characters, taste the food, and take these into your own kitchen and feel inspired.

Sadly, I have now sold and left my café but I take with me the fondest memories, especially of people and their terrific support and loyalty. So, my deepest thanks go to the people of Westmere and beyond for making 'Garnet Road' a very special place to be.

FOR MY MOTHER, LORAINE, AND MY FATHER,
BRIAN, WITH LOVE AND HAPPY MEMORIES OF
GROWING UP IN GARNET ROAD

4 oz's = 1 cup.

A VERY ELEGANT STATEMENT

Lemon, Balsamic Oyster Shooters

1 SMALL FOOD

First courses, antipasti, tapas, mezze, hors d'oeuvres, call them what you will – small food is a great way to eat. Traditionally these light and delicate morsels are an appetite-stimulating introduction to a meal. Now in true café style, small food is often eaten as an alternative to a conventional meal. Small food can be served in many ways; it makes perfect cocktail party food, a great mixed feast at lunch or suppertime, or an ultimate savoury 'snack' food. Naturally these dishes can still be served traditionally as a first taste, an evocative prelude to other courses.

LEMON, BALSAMIC OYSTER SHOOTERS

Make a very elegant statement – pass around oyster shooters on a tray and allow guests to 'drink' this appealing appetiser.

20 shot glasses

20 freshly shucked Pacific or Bluff oysters

¼–½ cup good quality aged balsamic vinegar

3 tblsp lemon-infused olive oil

1 Place 1 well-chilled oyster into each shot glass. Drizzle each with a little balsamic vinegar and a couple of drops of lemon-infused olive oil.

2 Pass around shot glasses on a tray or serve individually at the table.

Makes 20 shots

CHILLI BASIL PRAWNS

Kaffir limes are unusual in that the leaves are eaten and not the fruit of the trees. Kaffir lime is used a lot in Thai cuisine and the leaves can be found in Asian markets.

2 tblsp vegetable oil

20 green king prawns, peeled and deveined, leaving tails intact

1 tblsp grated fresh ginger

½ cup lime juice

1 tblsp fish sauce

2 tblsp sweet chilli sauce

10 large basil leaves

2 kaffir lime leaves, thinly sliced (optional)

1 Heat a frying pan and add oil and prawns. Stir-fry prawns for 1 minute.

2 Add remaining ingredients, tossing the prawns in liquid for 2–3 minutes until cooked. Alternatively, the prawns can be marinated in the dressing and then grilled or even barbecued.

3 Serve immediately.

Makes 20 finger-food portions

CHICKEN LIVERS with ANCHOVIES

The addition of anchovies to the creamy richness of chicken livers creates a magical combination.

2 tblsp olive oil

1 small onion, very finely chopped

4 anchovies

125 g chicken livers, cleaned

¼ cup brandy

75 g butter, melted

juice and finely grated zest of
 ½ lemon

sea salt

freshly ground black pepper

1 In a frying pan sweat onion in olive oil for 10 minutes until soft. Stir in anchovies, breaking them into a paste. Add livers chopped into chunks and brown briefly so that they retain some pink colouring.

2 Add brandy, butter, lemon juice and zest, and cook until liquid has evaporated. Season to taste with salt and pepper. Serve hot or cold on fresh bread or crostini or as part of a mixed plate.

Makes 20 small portions

LONG COOKED BROCCOLI and CAPERS

I had read several recipes for this amazing dish but couldn't quite believe it would be so good until I tasted it. Leanne Kitchen, an extremely talented chef and good friend, gave me my first opportunity to eat this most extraordinary comestible and I thank her for this and many other supremely memorable meals.

⅓ cup extra virgin olive oil

500 g broccoli, finely chopped

4 cloves garlic, crushed

juice of 1 lemon

¼ cup capers

2½ cups vegetable or chicken stock

salt and pepper

1 Heat oil in a saucepan, add remaining ingredients and bring to the boil. Cover and simmer very gently for 1 hour.

2 Remove covering and cook until liquid has evaporated. Stir regularly to break up broccoli. Serve hot or cold as an antipasto or vegetable dish.

Makes 20 small portions

INDONESIAN FISH CAKES with SWEET DIPPING SAUCE

It may be advisable to make a double batch of these moist and tasty fish cakes, as it is incredibly easy to eat a lot of them.

3 tsp coriander seeds

1 tsp cumin seeds

600 g white fish, boned and cubed

4 cloves garlic, crushed

2 cm piece fresh ginger, grated

2 small chillies, finely chopped

3 tblsp lime or lemon juice

¾ cup ground almonds

1 tsp salt

1 egg white

peanut or vegetable oil for frying

fresh lime wedges to serve

Dipping sauce:

¼ cup fish sauce

¼ cup light soya sauce

¼ cup water

¼ cup lime juice

¼ cup sweet chilli sauce

¼ cup palm or brown sugar

¼ cup chopped fresh coriander

1. Toast the coriander and cumin seeds and grind in a spice mill or pestle and mortar.
2. Toss all ingredients together except the egg white and limes and marinate in a non-metallic bowl covered with plastic wrap for 4–12 hours.
3. Place the marinated mixture and 1 egg white into the bowl of a food processor and pulse until a chunky paste is formed.
4. Form tablespoonful lots into little cakes and shallow fry in peanut oil for 1–2 minutes on each side. Drain on paper towels.
5. Serve with dipping sauce and fresh lime wedges.

Makes about 30 small fish cakes

Dipping sauce:
1. Blend all ingredients together until sugar has dissolved.

Makes 1 ½ cups

CRISP POTATOES with PORCINI RELISH

This is a sublime combination. The topping literally melts into the hot crisp potato bases and their warmth causes the porcini relish to release its essence and distinctive flavour.

750 g even-sized, washed baby potatoes

Porcini relish:

1-2 tblsp olive oil

1 red onion, very finely diced

1 clove garlic, crushed

50 g porcini, soaked in 1 cup warm water for 30 minutes

1 tblsp brown sugar

2 tblsp truffle oil

sea salt

freshly ground black pepper

1 Parboil potatoes. Slice into 1½ cm thick slices. Brush with olive oil and sprinkle with a little salt. Bake in an oven heated to 200°C for about 10 minutes until crisp and golden brown.

2 Serve topped with small mounds of porcini relish.

Porcini relish:

1 In a pan over low heat, sweat onion and garlic in olive oil for 10 minutes until soft.

2 Drain and lightly chop the porcini, add to the pan and cook for 5 minutes with the lid on. Strain the soaking liquid through a fine sieve and add to the pan with the brown sugar. Simmer gently until the liquid has almost evaporated. Remove to cool.

3 Once cold, stir in the truffle oil and season with salt and pepper to taste. Porcini relish improves on standing and will last stored in the refrigerator for about 3 weeks.

Makes 30 finger-food portions

THE TOPPING LITERALLY MELTS INTO
THE HOT CRISP POTATO BASES

Crisp Potatoes with Porcini Relish

SKEWERED GREEK LAMB SAUSAGES

If you've ever been to Greece and eaten lamb cooked on a skewer then these lamb sausages will bring back evocative memories of humble but worthy food and long, warm, gentle days.

500 g minced lamb

4 cloves garlic, crushed

3 tblsp olive oil

1 tsp ground cinnamon

finely grated zest of 1 lemon

1 tblsp fennel seeds, toasted

1 tsp salt

1 tsp ground black pepper

1   Mix all ingredients together well. With damp hands, shape into little sausages 3cm long and 1cm in diameter.

2   Fry gently in hot oil until brown on all sides and cooked through.

3   Skewer and serve warm with tzatziki dip (see page 24).

Makes 20 finger-food portions

TUNA TARTARE

Salmon also works well in this unusual and delightfully flavoured rendition of raw fish.

300 g very fresh raw tuna

3 gherkins, finely diced

3 tblsp capers

3 anchovy fillets, finely chopped

3 tblsp chopped fresh chives

1 tblsp chopped fresh mint

juice of 1 lemon

1 tblsp extra virgin olive oil

1 tblsp Worcestershire sauce

sea salt

freshly ground black pepper

1   Cut tuna into very small dice. Combine with remaining ingredients and chill to serve.

2   Serve small amounts with rye bread or crostini.

Makes about 20 small portions

Skewered Greek Lamb Sausages
with Tzatziki Dip

Black Olive and
Chickpea Purée, Roasted
Root Vegetable Purée and
Feta and Fennel Seed Dip

2 DIPS

Dipping into unctuous pastes of sometimes simple, other times wildly exotic ingredients is a sensual delight. Bread and dips can hold their own place as an item on any café menu but dips also cleverly form a base for other dishes. I have developed many inventive uses for dips and they play an intriguing role in the café kitchen. Fragrant with all that is ground into them and packed full of intense flavour, a good dip added in the right way will enhance a simple dish, lifting it to a higher culinary level. By always having some prepared dips on hand in the fridge you will be able to cope with any catering emergency. Experiment by adding appropriate dips to soups, stews, stuffings, pasta, noodles, salad dressings and classic sauces.

ROASTED ROOT VEGETABLE PURÉE

Any combination of roasted root vegetables would work in this dip but orange-coloured ones lend it a particularly attractive colour.

¼ **small pumpkin, peeled and cubed**

1 large carrot, peeled and cubed

1 large parsnip, peeled and cubed

6 cloves garlic, peeled

1 tsp cumin seeds

1 tsp paprika

½ **cup olive oil**

sea salt

freshly ground black pepper

1 Preheat oven to 180°C. Place prepared vegetables and garlic cloves into a roasting pan. Sprinkle over spices and drizzle over olive oil. Roast for 30 minutes or until vegetables are soft and caramelised. Remove to cool.

2 Once cold, purée vegetables and oil in a food processor to form a smooth paste, adding more oil if necessary to thin. Season to taste with salt and pepper.

Makes about 3 cups

FETA and FENNEL SEED DIP

Cooking is an eclectic art and we all gather favourite recipes from friends, working kitchens, eating out experiences and work-mates. Jennifer LeComte is a brilliant, bold and generous chef and I thoroughly enjoyed the years I spent cooking with her in her own café kitchen. This is a popular recipe of hers from that crucial time.

200 g feta cheese, crumbled

¾ cup sour cream

2 tblsp fennel seeds, toasted

3 tblsp extra virgin olive oil

1 Cream together feta and sour cream to form a smooth paste. Stir in fennel seeds and olive oil.

2 Serve as a dip for vegetables or spread on crostini or crackers.

Makes about 2 cups

BLACK OLIVE and CHICKPEA PURÉE

The ancient and salty flavour of olives thoughtfully enhances this creamy chickpea purée.

1 cup chickpeas

2 bay leaves

4 cloves garlic, peeled

½ cup pitted Kalamata olives

juice of 3 lemons

⅓ cup extra virgin olive oil

sea salt

freshly ground black pepper

1 Soak chickpeas overnight in plenty of cold water.

2 Drain chickpeas, place in a saucepan with the bay leaves and cover with fresh cold water. Bring to the boil then simmer for 1 hour until tender. Drain and allow to cool.

3 Crush garlic in the bowl of a food processor. Add pitted olives and chickpeas and pulse to chop. Add lemon juice and olive oil and process well to combine. Season to taste with salt and pepper. Adjust juice or oil if necessary for taste and texture.

Makes about 2 cups

CLASSIC BASIL PESTO

Mention pesto and the first one to come to mind no doubt would be classic basil pesto.

2 bunches basil (about 2 well-packed cups)

2 cloves garlic

¼ cup Parmesan

¼ cup pinenuts

½ cup olive oil

salt to taste

1. Prepare ingredients: remove basil leaves from stems. Peel garlic cloves. Grate, crumble or slice Parmesan. Toast pinenuts if preferred – this changes their flavour, freshens them and adds even more nuttiness.
2. Place basil and garlic cloves into the bowl of a food processor and pulse to chop.
3. Add Parmesan and pinenuts. Blend to a pulp.
4. With motor running, drizzle in olive oil, scrape down sides, and process to form a smooth paste. Adjust seasoning to taste.

Makes about 1 cup

RED PESTO

Based on the premise that pesto is essentially a ground paste, this vivid red dip is a play on the classic original.

2 cloves garlic

¼ cup basil leaves

3 red peppers, roasted

½ cup sun-dried tomatoes

¼ cup tomato paste

¼ cup extra virgin olive oil

1 tsp sugar

salt and pepper

1. Place garlic into the bowl of a food processor and pulse to chop. Add basil, red peppers, sun-dried tomatoes and tomato paste. Process to purée.
2. Add oil to amalgamate, and sugar, salt and pepper to taste.

Makes about 2 cups

WHITE FISH PATÉ

Voluptuously creamy and yet textured and with a most delicate fish flavour, this paté is more in the style of rillettes.

50 g butter, softened

100 g cream cheese

250 g cooked white fish, skin and bones removed

2 tblsp sour cream

1 tblsp lemon juice

few drops Tabasco sauce

pinch freshly grated nutmeg

sea salt

1 Cream together butter and cream cheese. Mash fish with a fork to break up. Gently mix fish, sour cream, lemon juice and seasonings into creamed mixture.

2 Serve lightly chilled with Melba toast or crostini and caperberries or capers.

Makes about 2 cups

GREEN OLIVE CREAM

I like this extraordinary combination of tart and salty mixed with cool and sour. Green olive cream becomes even more exceptional served with hot bread or over grilled fish or chicken.

1 cup pitted green olives

2 cloves garlic

2 tblsp chopped parsley

2 tblsp lemon juice

2 tblsp extra virgin olive oil

1 cup sour cream

sea salt

black pepper

1 Place olives, garlic and parsley into the bowl of a food processor and pulse to chop. Add lemon juice, oil and sour cream and process to a smooth cream. Adjust seasoning with salt and pepper to taste.

Makes about 2 cups

VOLUPTUOUSLY CREAMY

White Fish Paté

GREEK TZATZIKI

Warm pita bread and Kalamata olives are the obvious accompaniments to this Greek dip and make a sublime combination to which little more is necessary. Tzatziki also works well as a sauce with grilled fish or meat.

½ telegraph cucumber, seeded but unpeeled

1 cup Greek yoghurt, or thick yoghurt

3 cloves garlic, crushed

1 tblsp chopped fresh dill

1 tblsp chopped fresh basil

2 tblsp extra virgin olive oil

juice of 1 lemon

salt

1 Very finely dice cucumber and place on paper towels to release excess juice.

2 Mix all ingredients together and season with salt to taste. Chill well to serve.

Makes about 2 cups

LIPTAUER CHEESE DIP

Cheese logs, which were often rather strange and not always very good, seemed to feature in a certain period of New Zealand entertaining culture. This is not one of them! Liptauer is an extremely palatable combination of cheeses mixed with spirited extras. It should be served heaped up next to some crusty bread and never in the form of a log.

50 g butter

½ cup cream cheese

½ cup sour cream

½ cup grated aged Cheddar

¼ cup finely diced gherkins

2 tblsp chopped chives

1 tblsp wholegrain mustard

juice of 1 lemon

1 tsp paprika

¼ tsp chilli powder

sea salt

freshly ground black pepper

1 Cream butter with cream cheese and sour cream. Beat in grated Cheddar and remaining ingredients. Adjust seasoning with salt and pepper to taste.

Makes about 2 cups

3 SOUPS

Soups capture and combine the true essence of ingredients to form a nurturing liquid meal. By following a few basic rules mixed with a little pure good sense, good soups are highly achievable. Important soup rules include not adding odds and ends from the fridge such as sad old vegetables, as the final taste will only be as good as the quality of the ingredients used. Good stocks make the most generous flavour additions possible, but try to use appropriately flavoured stocks. If onions are required as a base, be certain to sweat them long and slow so that they release as much flavour as possible into the soup. Likewise, simmer soups to extract the most flavour from ingredients. Season soups at the end of cooking as reduction of liquid changes and concentrates flavours. Taste, texture and balance are all important so don't try to be too clever and combine too many flavours.

KUMARA and CORIANDER SOUP

Cameron Woodcock, a chef with serious style and ability, created this soup for the Garnet Road soup lovers, and it has been a great hit.

4 tblsp vegetable oil

2 large onions, peeled and diced

1 cm piece fresh ginger, grated

4 large kumara (sweet potatoes)

6 cups chicken or vegetable stock

1 cup coconut cream

½ cup chopped fresh coriander

salt and pepper

1   In a large saucepan sweat onions and ginger in oil until softened but not coloured. Add kumara and stock and bring to the boil. Simmer gently until kumara is very tender. Add coconut cream, coriander, salt and pepper to taste.

2   Purée in a blender or food processor. Gently reheat through. Adjust seasoning if necessary.

Serves 6

HOT and SOUR GLASS NOODLE SOUP

While this is not one of Ray McVinnie's actual recipes, it is a style of soup that will forever remind me of the pleasures of working with him. Ray is exceptionally knowledgeable about Asian ingredients, an inspired chef and loads of fun. Thanks, Ray, for such stimulating times in the café kitchen.

6 cups good quality chicken stock

2 stalks lemongrass, peeled and crushed

2 cm piece ginger, peeled and grated

250 g glass vermicelli (also known as cellophane or beanthread noodles)

½ cup sliced snow peas

1 head bok choy, trimmed

2 red chillies, finely sliced

4 tblsp fresh lime juice

3 tblsp roughly torn coriander leaves

1   Place stock, lemongrass and ginger into a large saucepan and bring to the boil to infuse flavours. Boil for 5 minutes then strain to remove lemongrass and ginger. Return stock to the pan.

2   Add noodles and vegetables and simmer for 2 minutes to cook. Lastly add chilli and lime juice. Serve garnished with coriander.

Serves 6

SMOKED FISH SOUP

Often a simple dish will capture our hearts and become cherished in our culinary reminiscences. This one does it for me every time.

75 g butter

1 onion, chopped

2 cloves garlic, crushed

4 tblsp plain flour

2½ cups milk

2½ cups fish or vegetable stock

600 g smoked fish, flaked

3 tblsp chopped parsley

sea salt

freshly ground black pepper

1   In a large saucepan sweat onion and garlic in melted butter until softened but not coloured. Stir in flour and cook for 1 minute. Gradually add milk and stock, stirring continually over heat until sauce thickens.

2   Add smoked fish and parsley. Cook until fish is heated through. Season to taste with salt and pepper.

Serves 6

Hot and Sour Glass Noodle Soup

ROAST RED PEPPER and AUBERGINE SOUP

The initial roasting of the vegetables gives this soup an extra intensity of flavour.

3 red peppers, halved and seeds removed

1 large aubergine or 2 smaller ones

3 tblsp olive oil

1 onion, diced

400 g can Italian peeled tomatoes, crushed

3 cups chicken or vegetable stock

2 tblsp tomato paste

sea salt

freshly ground black pepper

2 tblsp shredded fresh basil

1   Preheat oven to 180°C. Rub peppers and aubergine with a little oil and place in a roasting pan. Roast peppers for 30 minutes and aubergine for 45-60 minutes until soft when squeezed. Remove to cool.

2   Skin the peppers and chop roughly. Cut the aubergine in half lengthways, scoop out flesh and chop roughly. Discard skin.

3   In a large saucepan sweat onion in remaining oil until softened. Add peppers, aubergine, tomatoes, stock and tomato paste. Bring to the boil then simmer for 15 minutes to reduce.

4   Purée in a blender or food processor. Season to taste with salt and pepper. Reheat and serve with shredded fresh basil leaves.

Serves 6

LEEK and POTATO SOUP of SUBSTANCE

This is a soup with lots of body and texture. It can, of course, be made smooth but I prefer to retain some good chunks of leek and potato. To clean leeks efficiently, slice them first and then wash them well. Using this method, any extra stubborn dirt will be easily removed.

2 tblsp olive oil

2 tblsp butter

1 large onion, peeled and chopped

4 cloves garlic, peeled and chopped

3 large potatoes, peeled and evenly chopped

3 leeks, thinly sliced and well washed

6 cups vegetable or chicken stock

½ cup sour cream

sea salt

freshly ground black pepper

1   In a large saucepan sweat onions and garlic in oil and butter until translucent.

2   Add potatoes, leeks and stock. Bring to the boil then simmer until potatoes are tender. Purée half the soup mixture, adding the sour cream. Leave half the mixture as is to retain texture.

3   Combine both mixtures. Season to taste with salt and pepper.

Serves 6

Roast Red Pepper and
Aubergine Soup

ALL SORTS OF WARMING MEMORIES

Ham, Barley and Spinach Soup

HAM, BARLEY and SPINACH SOUP

Once made you will find that good soup will stir up all sorts of warming memories.

3 tblsp olive oil

1 onion, peeled and diced

1 carrot, peeled and diced

2 sticks celery, diced

1 ham bone or 2 bacon hocks

1 cup barley

2 bay leaves

2 cups shredded washed spinach

sea salt

freshly ground black pepper

1 In a large saucepan sweat diced onion, carrot and celery in oil for 10 minutes to soften without browning. Add ham bone or hocks, barley and bay leaves. Generously cover with cold water and bring to the boil. Simmer uncovered for 1 hour.

2 Remove bay leaves and bones but return any shreds of meat to the saucepan. Add spinach and cook for a couple of minutes to wilt spinach. Season with salt and pepper to taste.

Serves 4

MEDITERRANEAN PUMPKIN and SMOKED PAPRIKA SOUP

Spanish smoked paprika has a totally different flavour to the more common Hungarian paprika that we all know. It has an out-of-this-world smoky aroma and taste that comes from the smoking process of the pimenton (peppers). It is available in most good delicatessens and specialty food stores. Look out for it and use it – you won't be disappointed.

3 tblsp olive oil

3 tblsp butter

1 onion, peeled

½ large crown pumpkin, peeled, seeds removed

1 potato, peeled

1 carrot, peeled

2 tomatoes

6 cups vegetable or chicken stock

1 tblsp tomato paste

2 tsp Spanish sweet smoked paprika

sea salt

freshly ground black pepper

1 Cut all vegetables into large dice.

2 In a large saucepan sweat onion in oil and butter until translucent. Add all the vegetables, stock and tomato paste and bring to the boil. Simmer uncovered until vegetables are very tender.

3 Purée in a blender or food processor, adding paprika and salt and pepper to season. Thin with a little extra stock if necessary.

4 Reheat gently to serve.

Serves 6

4 LIGHT MEALS

Light meals typify essential café fare and probably comprise the greatest proportion of foods prepared in any café. A simple but tasty repast is all many customers need in the middle of the day when they are short on time or low on energy. As these dishes are not substantial, they need to be bold and hold heightened flavours to give that much-needed hit. A café provides the perfect setting to nibble a tasty treat and be swept away by the visual panorama of life bustling by. There's always gossip to be overheard, business deals to complete, lovers to observe casually, jokes and laughter to share. All these scenes abound and attract but ultimately the food and coffee have to be the most enticing elements on offer.

TUSCAN PRESSED SANDWICHES

Allow 1 small loaf or roll per person or make 1 large loaf by the same method and slice into individual wedges. Go wild with your own choice of filling ingredients and combinations.

small rustic loaves of bread

extra virgin olive oil

assorted filling ingredients, for example:

sliced ham or pastrami

sliced chicken or turkey

smoked salmon

sliced cheese

char-grilled aubergine, peppers or zucchini

dips or chutney

ricotta cheese

lettuce, rocket or basil leaves

sliced tomato or cucumber, drained on paper towels

1 Cut loaves in half and pull out most of the doughy interior. Take care not to break the crusts. Drizzle hollowed-out crusts with extra virgin olive oil.

2 Layer chosen filling ingredients to fill inside of loaves well. Replace tops on each loaf. Wrap in plastic wrap and place a weight firmly onto each and leave to press for several hours.

3 Remove weights and wrapping and slice sandwiches to serve.

Serves any number of people

GO WILD WITH YOUR OWN CHOICE
OF FILLING INGREDIENTS
Tuscan Pressed Sandwiches

GROUND BEEF LOAVES in SAGE BREAD

These make very hearty snacks. A particularly enjoyable twist is that the aromatic flavour of sage comes through beautifully in the encapsulating bread.

Sage bread dough:

½ cup warm water

1 tsp sugar

2 tsp active dried yeast

2½ cups plain flour

1 tsp salt

2 tblsp chopped fresh sage

2 large eggs

100 g butter, softened

Ground beef:

3 tblsp olive oil

1 onion, finely chopped

2 cloves garlic, crushed

500 g ground beef mince

1 tsp Tabasco sauce

3 tblsp tomato paste

1 tblsp chopped fresh parsley

1 tblsp chopped fresh oregano

sea salt

freshly ground black pepper

1 egg yolk to glaze

1   To make bread dough, place water into a small bowl and sprinkle with sugar and yeast. Leave in a warm place for 5 minutes for yeast to activate and become foamy.

2   Place flour, salt and sage into a large bowl and make a well in the centre. Place egg, butter and activated yeast mixture into well. Mix with a wooden spoon to bring together into a firm dough. Place in a lightly oiled bowl, cover with plastic wrap and leave until doubled in size (takes about 45 minutes).

3   Punch down risen dough. Use as required.

Ground beef:

4   In a frying pan sweat onion and garlic in oil until softened. Add beef and cook until browned. Add flavourings and season with salt and pepper. Cook for a further 5 minutes to concentrate flavours. Remove to cool. Grease 8 mini loaf tins or large muffin pans.

5   Divide prepared dough into 8 portions. Roll out each to 3 mm thick. Divide beef equally and place in the centre of each piece of dough. Bring up edges of dough to cover filling and fit bundles into prepared tins. Cover with a clean damp cloth and leave until dough has doubled in size.

6   Heat oven to 180ºC. Glaze dough with beaten egg yolk mixed with a little water. Bake for 25-30 minutes until golden brown.

Makes 8

SAUSAGES in SAGE BREAD

It never ceases to amaze me how many people have fond recollections of classic sausage rolls. This could be called a delicious modern play on that Kiwi icon.

1 quantity sage bread dough (see Ground Beef Loaves opposite)

8 flavoursome sausages, par-boiled

1 egg yolk to glaze

1   Roll out dough to 3 mm thick. Cut 2 cm thick strips and wrap around sausages. Place on a lightly oiled baking tray, cover with a clean damp cloth and leave until dough has doubled in size.

2   Heat oven to 180ºC. Glaze dough with beaten egg yolk mixed with a little water. Bake for 20 minutes until golden brown. Serve with a favourite chutney.

Makes 8

SAVOURY BREAD and BUTTER CAKE

Here's a chance to experiment with different combinations of filling ingredients in the layers of this savoury bread and butter cake.

10 slices white sandwich bread

100 g butter, softened

2 cups cooked vegetables of choice

¼ cup chopped fresh basil

1 cup grated Cheddar cheese

sliced ham or other meat (optional)

6 large eggs

2½ cups milk

½ cup cream

sea salt

freshly ground black pepper

1   Grease a 20 cm spring-form cake tin. Butter bread and layer in prepared tin alternating with selected vegetables, herbs, cheese and meat if desired. Press down well. Make sure top layer of bread is attractively arranged.

2   Beat eggs, milk and cream together and season well with salt and pepper. Pour evenly over cake and leave to rest for half an hour for bread to absorb liquid completely. Preheat oven to 150ºC.

3   Cover with cooking foil and bake for 30 minutes. Remove foil and bake for a further 30 minutes. Cake will inflate slightly when cooked, deflating again once cold. Allow to cool a little before removing from tin.

Serves 8

Pesto, Feta and Tomato
Freeform Tarts

PESTO, FETA and TOMATO FREEFORM TARTS

Pre-rolled pastry sheets are a real bonus when you're in a hurry and they cut into 4 to produce pastries of just the right size.

2 sheets pre-rolled puff pastry

8 tblsp basil pesto (see page 21)

2 tomatoes, sliced

100 g feta, crumbled

8 black olives

1   Heat oven to 190ºC.

2   Cut each sheet of pastry into 4 squares and place onto a lightly oiled baking tray. Score a 1 cm frame around the edge of each pastry square.

3   Divide filling ingredients between squares, layering with pesto, feta, a slice of tomato and an olive.

4   Bake pastries for 15-20 minutes until edges are puffed and golden brown.

Makes 8

PUMPKIN, CHORIZO AND FETA FRITTATA

Many people are complimentary about this frittata, which can be varied enormously by changing the filling ingredients. Finishing the frittata in the oven produces a good effect and makes for easy cutting and serving in the café. The same recipe can be used to make individual frittatas, which are also well received.

300g pumpkin, peeled and cubed

¼ cup olive oil

1 onion, peeled and sliced

8 eggs

1 cup cream

salt and pepper

2 chorizo, sliced (or any spicy sausage)

1 tblsp chopped fresh thyme

1 tblsp chopped fresh parsley

100 g crumbled feta

1   Preheat oven to 170ºC. Boil or steam pumpkin until tender. Drain and set aside.

2   In a 24 cm non-stick frying pan with an ovenproof handle, sweat onion in 2 tblsp olive oil until softened.

3   Beat eggs with cream and season well with salt and pepper. Mix in pumpkin, onion, chorizo and herbs.

4   Place remaining oil in same frying pan over heat. Once hot, pour in frittata mixture. Stir briefly to distribute ingredients evenly. Top with crumbled feta. Bake for 45 minutes or until set.

5   Remove from oven and allow to cool a little before inverting onto a plate to turn out. Flip back to presentation side to serve.

Serves 8

Risotto, Ricotta and
Spinach Cakes

RISOTTO, RICOTTA and SPINACH CAKES

Originally this appeared in the café as one large cake served cut into slices. In my study of people's eating habits I have discovered that most rather enjoy separate food items so these are now served as individual cakes and are incredibly popular.

4 tblsp olive oil

1 onion, finely diced

3 cloves garlic, crushed

1 cup Italian risotto rice

2½ cups hot vegetable or chicken stock

1 cup ricotta

½ cup cream or milk

1 cup chopped blanched spinach

2 tblsp chopped fresh basil

1 cup grated Cheddar cheese

½ cup grated Parmesan

6 eggs, lightly beaten

sea salt

freshly ground black pepper

2 tblsp dried breadcrumbs

1 Heat a heavy-based saucepan or risotto pan and sweat onion and garlic in oil over a medium heat. Add risotto rice and allow to toast but not brown, stirring continuously for 2 minutes. Add hot stock all at once and a little salt and pepper. Bring to the boil, stir, then cover and simmer for 15 minutes. Turn out into a bowl to cool.

2 Mix remaining ingredients into cold risotto and season well with salt and pepper.

3 Preheat oven to 180ºC. Grease and dust with breadcrumbs 10–12 individual large muffin tins or one 22 cm spring-form cake tin. Fill mixture into tins. Bake small cakes for about 30 minutes depending on size, large cake for 1¼ hours or until a knife inserted in the centre comes out clean.

Serves 8–10

GOUGÈRES with SMOKED SALMON

Gougères are savoury choux flavoured with cheese and can be served as an entrée or light meal. In Burgundy, cold gougères traditionally accompany wine-tasting in cellars.

Choux pastry:

1 cup plain flour

pinch salt

1 cup water

100 g butter, cubed

1 tsp Dijon mustard

3 large eggs, lightly beaten

½ cup grated Gruyère cheese

Filling:

½ cup sour cream

2 tblsp chopped fresh dill or chives

sea salt

freshly ground black pepper

200 g sliced smoked salmon

small bunch of rocket leaves

1   Sift flour and salt onto a piece of paper. Place the water and butter into a saucepan and heat until butter melts. Bring to a rolling boil then shoot in flour all at once, quickly remove from the heat and beat to bring mixture together. Turn into a bowl to cool a little.

2   Beat in mustard, then egg in small amounts. Continue beating until mixture is very glossy. Stir in cheese.

3   Preheat oven to 190ºC. Lightly grease a baking tray.

4   Place mounded spoonfuls onto baking tray. Sprinkle with cold water to create steam. Bake for 25 minutes until puffed, dry and golden brown.

5   Once cold, slit in half and fill with a little sour cream mixed with dill or chives, slices of salmon seasoned with salt and pepper, and rocket leaves.

Makes 15

IN BURGUNDY, COLD GOUGÈRES TRADITIONALLY
ACCOMPANY WINE-TASTING IN CELLARS

Gougères with Smoked Salmon

5 SALADS

Well composed or spontaneously tossed, salads are favourites for casual entertaining. Interesting salad combinations can be made ahead and stashed in the fridge to make catering easy. Many of these salads improve upon standing so can easily be made a day in advance. A truly amazing and versatile invention, salad can double as an entrée, a side dish, a main course and then fruit salad, of course, makes a great breakfast dish or dessert. Who would have thought that one concept could offer so much? It's quite overwhelming when you think of it. These recipes are also overwhelming in their array of flavour combinations but not in their composure. You will find them uncomplicated to replicate and yet stimulating to the senses to consume.

LEBANESE FATTOUSH

This humble but character-filled salad has to be dedicated to my wonderful Lebanese great-grandfather, Samuel Bishara, who I never met but oh so wish I had. Sumac is a pungent, astringent spice ground from the purple berries of a decorative bush peculiar to the Middle East. It is worth finding but not essential to the finished salad.

2 large, stale pita breads

1 telegraph cucumber, seeds removed

4 ripe tomatoes, seeds removed

1 red onion, peeled

¼ cup chopped fresh parsley

¼ cup chopped fresh coriander

¼ cup chopped fresh mint

sea salt

freshly ground black pepper

2 tsp sumac (optional)

Lemon dressing:

3 cloves garlic, crushed

¼ cup lemon juice

¼ cup extra virgin olive oil

1 Preheat oven to 180ºC. Tear pita bread roughly into 2 cm pieces and spread over a baking tray. Bake for 5–10 minutes until golden and crisp. Remove to cool.

2 Dice cucumber, tomato flesh and onion and combine in a bowl with herbs and crisp pita pieces. Season well with salt and pepper.

3 Blend dressing ingredients together, pour over salad and toss well to coat. Sprinkle with sumac if available. Don't worry if you cannot procure sumac, the salad will still be delicious.

Serves 8

DEDICATED TO MY WONDERFUL LEBANESE
GREAT-GRANDFATHER, SAMUEL BISHARA

Lebanese Fattoush

MOZZARELLA, TOMATO and OLIVE SALAD with ROASTED GARLIC DRESSING

This unusual roasted garlic dressing embellishes an obviously Italian salad.

2 cups bocconcini (baby balls of fresh mozzarella)

2 cups cherry tomatoes

½ cup quality small olives

½ cup roughly torn basil leaves

Dressing:

1 whole head of garlic

juice of 2 lemons

¼ cup extra virgin olive oil

1 tsp sugar

sea salt

freshly ground black pepper

1   Preheat oven to 180ºC. Cut garlic head in half, wrap in foil and place in a small oven pan. Roast for 40 minutes until very soft. Remove and cool.

2   Squeeze to remove garlic pulp. Blend garlic with remaining dressing ingredients and season with salt and pepper to taste.

3   Place salad ingredients into a bowl. Pour over dressing and toss well to combine.

Serves 8

ORZO with MUSHROOMS, GARLIC and ROCKET

Orzo, a delicate rice-shaped pasta, is becoming more readily available but, of course, any other pasta could be substituted for orzo in this recipe.

1½ cups orzo

500 g button mushrooms

5 cloves garlic, crushed

¼ cup extra virgin olive oil

4 tblsp balsamic vinegar

sea salt

freshly ground black pepper

2 good handfuls of rocket

1   Cook orzo in plenty of boiling salted water until just tender. Drain, rinse in cold water and drain well.

2   Lightly fry mushrooms and garlic in olive oil. Remove and allow to cool in oil.

3   Combine orzo with balsamic vinegar, mushrooms, garlic and flavoured oil. Season to taste with salt and pepper. Toss through rocket and serve.

Serves 6

Mozzarella, Tomato and Olive
Salad with Roasted Garlic Dressing

WONDERFUL, ALMOST NUTTY FLAVOUR

Roasted Cauliflower with
Caper Crumbs

ROASTED CAULIFLOWER with CAPER CRUMBS

Roasting the cauliflower gives it a wonderful, almost nutty flavour.

1 good-sized cauliflower

½ cup coarsely crumbled stale bread

¼ cup capers

4 cloves garlic, crushed

¼ cup olive oil

4 tblsp chopped fresh parsley

¼ cup pinenuts, lightly toasted

¼ cup sun-dried tomatoes, roughly chopped

sea salt

freshly ground black pepper

1 Preheat oven to 170ºC. Cut cauliflower into even-sized small florets.

2 Place cauliflower, crumbled bread and capers into an oven pan. Pour over crushed garlic and oil mixed together and toss well to coat. Roast for about 30 minutes, stirring occasionally to allow for even cooking until golden brown. Remove to cool.

3 Toss together with parsley, pinenuts and sun-dried tomatoes. Season with salt and pepper to taste.

Serves 4-6

BARLEY SALAD with TOMATO DRESSING

Barley has a wonderful nutty taste and creamy texture, which makes it an astounding base for a salad.

2 cups pearl barley

2 bay leaves

¼ cup olive oil

1 onion, sliced

4 cloves garlic, crushed

400 g can peeled tomatoes, crushed

3 tblsp balsamic vinegar

1 tblsp brown sugar

sea salt

freshly ground black pepper

1 Place barley and bay leaves into a large saucepan. Cover with cold water and bring to the boil. Simmer for 45 minutes or until barley is cooked. Drain well and remove bay leaves.

2 Meanwhile, in another saucepan, sweat onion and garlic in oil until softened. Add tomatoes and simmer for 10-15 minutes to form a thick sauce. Add balsamic vinegar, brown sugar and salt and pepper to taste.

3 Mix barley into tomato dressing. Allow to cool completely. Adjust seasoning if necessary before serving.

Serves 6-8

CRISPY NOODLE SALAD with CHILLI and SPRING ONION VINAIGRETTE

All sorts of colours, tastes and textures resonate in this wild and vibrant salad.

140 g packet Crispy Noodles

2 cups finely shredded red cabbage

1 cup mesclun (mixed baby salad greens)

1 carrot, peeled and cut into very fine strips

½ cup crunchy sprouts

Vinaigrette:

2 spring onions, finely minced

3 tblsp sweet chilli sauce

juice of 2 limes or lemons

1 tsp light soya sauce

1 tblsp sesame oil

2 tblsp peanut oil

1. Blend vinaigrette ingredients together.
2. Pour over combined salad ingredients and toss well.

Serves 6

BEETROOT with SOUR CREAM and HORSERADISH DRESSING

This salad turns out to be a fantastic pink colour, creating a little subterfuge for the exciting kick that horseradish gives the dressing.

1 kg beetroot

3 tblsp shredded fresh mint

Dressing:

½ cup sour cream

1–2 tblsp prepared horseradish cream

¼ cup extra virgin olive oil

juice and zest of 1 lemon

freshly ground black pepper

1. Boil the whole beetroot in plenty of water until tender. This may take up to an hour depending on the size of the beetroot. Drain and allow to cool then remove the skins – they should just slip off. Cut beetroot into chunks or slices.
2. Whisk the dressing ingredients together to combine, adding horseradish to taste. Toss through the beetroot. Arrange on a serving platter and scatter with shredded mint.

Serves 6-8

COLOURS, TASTES AND TEXTURES RESONATE
IN THIS WILD AND VIBRANT SALAD

Crispy Noodle Salad with Chilli and Spring Onion Vinaigrette

49

NORTH AFRICAN AUBERGINE SALAD

Piquant spices interfuse beautifully with the melt-in-your-mouth texture of roasted aubergine.

3 medium aubergines (approx. 750g)

olive oil to coat

1 tsp Spanish sweet smoked paprika

1 tsp ground cumin

1 tsp ground coriander

Dressing:

3 cloves garlic, crushed

3 tblsp extra virgin olive oil

zest and juice of 2 lemons

¼ cup roughly chopped fresh coriander leaves

sea salt

freshly ground black pepper

1 Preheat oven to 180ºC. Slice aubergines into half rounds 1 cm thick and brush lightly with olive oil. Mix spices together and rub into aubergine slices. Spread over an oven tray and roast for 20-25 minutes until golden brown. Remove to cool.

2 Mix garlic, measured oil, lemon juice and zest and coriander together. Toss through spiced aubergine. Season to taste with salt and pepper.

Serves 6-8

GREEN BEANS with PARSLEY DRESSING and CHERRY TOMATOES

A stunning colour and flavour combination. Trim the stalk end off the beans but leave the tails on because they are so pretty.

500 g green beans, trimmed

1 cup red cherry tomatoes

Parsley dressing:

2 cloves garlic, peeled

½ cup parsley sprigs

¼ cup extra virgin olive oil

sea salt

freshly ground black pepper

1 Cook beans in boiling salted water until just tender. Drain and refresh in ice-cold water. Drain and dry.

2 In the bowl of a food processor purée garlic, parsley and olive oil together to make a dressing. Season with salt and pepper to taste.

3 Toss beans well in dressing. Serve scattered with cherry tomatoes.

Serves 4

MELT-IN-YOUR-MOUTH TEXTURE
OF ROASTED AUBERGINE

Mixed salad plate: Carrot, Coconut and
Currant, Green Beans with
Parsley Dressing and Cherry
Tomatoes, North African
Aubergine, Hot Sweet Cucumber

HOT SWEET CUCUMBER SALAD

A nice clean salad to add to a mixed salad plate.

2 telegraph cucumbers, halved and
seeds removed

2 green chillies, finely sliced

zest and juice of 1 lime or lemon

2 tblsp sugar

2 tblsp fish sauce

Vietnamese mint leaves (or
ordinary mint)

1   With a vegetable peeler strip long ribbons down
the length of the cucumber halves and place in a
bowl.

2   Mix remaining ingredients together and pour over
cucumber. Toss well to combine.

Serves 4-6

CHAR-GRILLED CAESAR SALAD

Char-grilling the cos lettuce is a startling treatment for what still remains my most
favourite salad. Sue Fleischl, the great caterer of Auckland, acquainted me with this
clever twist on the classic Caesar salad, and it is a fun interpretation to try, especially
if you're having a barbecue.

2 heads cos lettuce

8 anchovies

4 slices bacon, diced and fried
until crisp

shaved Parmesan

Garlic croûtons:

3 slices white bread, crusts removed

¼ cup olive oil

2 cloves garlic, crushed

Dressing:

1 egg

2 anchovies

juice of 2 lemons

1 tsp Dijon mustard

1 tblsp Worcestershire sauce

sea salt

freshly ground black pepper

¼ cup extra virgin olive oil

1   To make the croûtons cut the bread into ½ cm
cubes. Mix oil and garlic together to infuse for as
long as possible then strain off the garlic. Heat
the garlic oil and shallow fry the bread cubes until
evenly golden brown. Drain on paper towels.

2   To make the dressing, very briefly poach the egg
then scoop into a food processor or bowl and
whisk with anchovies, lemon juice, mustard,
Worcestershire sauce, salt and pepper to taste.
Slowly drizzle in olive oil while whisking
constantly to amalgamate.

3   Heat a barbecue or char-grill and grill the cos
lettuce leaves briefly to scorch.

4   Assemble the salad by tossing cos with croûtons
in dressing. Scatter with anchovies and bacon if
desired and shavings of fresh Parmesan.

Serves 4-6

CARROT, COCONUT and CURRANT SALAD

An extremely simple salad but the delightful sweet and sour flavours lend it a mysterious complexity.

3 medium carrots, peeled

½ cup thread coconut

½ cup currants

1 tblsp sugar

1 tsp salt

¼ cup white wine vinegar

¼ cup vegetable oil

3 tblsp chopped fresh mint or coriander

1 Grate carrots and mix with coconut.

2 Sprinkle currants with sugar and salt then cover with vinegar and soak for 30 minutes. Pour over carrots and coconut. Add oil and toss well. Chill and serve topped with mint or coriander.

Serves 4-6

DRY-CURRIED BROCCOLI SALAD

Try cauliflower, potatoes or even carrots instead of the broccoli for a change.

1 kg broccoli, trimmed into florets

¼ cup vegetable oil

1 tsp mustard seeds

1 tsp cumin seeds

1 onion, finely diced

2 cloves garlic, crushed

2 cm piece fresh ginger, grated

1 green chilli, finely chopped

½ tsp turmeric

1 tsp ground coriander

juice of 1 lemon

½ tsp salt

½ cup plain yoghurt

¼ cup chopped fresh coriander leaves

½ tsp paprika

1 Blanch broccoli florets in boiling salted water for about 3 minutes until just tender. Drain and plunge into ice-cold water to cool. Drain well.

2 Heat oil in a large frying pan. Add mustard and cumin seeds and when they start to pop add onion, garlic, ginger, chilli, turmeric and coriander. Stir-fry for 2 minutes. Add lemon juice, salt and cooked broccoli. Stir-fry for another 2 minutes, tossing broccoli well to coat in spices. Remove to cool.

3 Serve topped with yoghurt, chopped coriander leaves and a dusting of paprika.

Serves 6

A TASTE AND TEXTURAL SENSATION

White Bean and Tuna Salad

WHITE BEAN and TUNA SALAD

The combination of buttery beans, crunchy vegetables, tons of garlic and tuna creates a taste and textural sensation.

1 cup dried white beans (haricot, cannelini or baby lima)

3 stalks celery, finely sliced

2 spring onions, finely sliced

1 red onion, finely diced

2 tblsp chopped fresh tarragon

1 cup drained and flaked canned tuna

Dressing:

3 tblsp cooked white beans

6 cloves garlic, crushed

½ cup extra virgin olive oil

juice of 3 lemons

sea salt

freshly ground black pepper

1   Soak beans overnight in cold water.

2   Next day, drain beans, place in a saucepan and cover with fresh cold water. Bring to the boil then simmer for 1 hour until beans are very tender. Drain and set aside to cool, reserving 3 tblsp of beans for dressing.

3   In a blender or food processor purée 3 tblsp cooked white beans with dressing ingredients, season with salt and pepper and pour over beans while still warm so that flavours are well absorbed. Cool completely then mix in remaining salad ingredients.

Serves 4

BABY POTATO SALAD with SWEET ONION DRESSING

Potato salad is still one of the most requested of all the café salad varieties.

1 kg washed baby potatoes, unpeeled

Sweet onion dressing:

2 red onions, finely diced

3 spring onions, finely sliced

2 cloves garlic, crushed

¼ cup balsamic vinegar

¼ cup extra virgin olive oil

1 tsp sugar

2 tblsp chopped fresh parsley

2 tblsp chopped fresh chives

sea salt

freshly ground black pepper

1   Cook potatoes in boiling salted water until just tender. Drain and dress while still warm then allow to cool.

2   Whisk dressing ingredients together and pour over warm potatoes.

Serves 6

SPINACH, SEAWEED and PICKLED GINGER SALAD

This light, crisp salad is a conglomeration of the most interesting and subtle flavours of Japanese ingredients.

1 good-sized bunch spinach, stalks removed

2 sheets nori seaweed

¼ cup Japanese pickled ginger

¼ cup wakame (optional)

3 tblsp sesame seeds, toasted

Japanese dressing:

¼ cup mirin (sweetened rice wine)

3 tblsp sesame oil

2 tblsp dark Japanese soya sauce

juice of 1 lemon

1   Wash and dry spinach and tear into pieces. Cut nori into strips. Roughly chop pickled ginger. Soak wakame in warm water for 1 minute to re-hydrate then drain. Toss these ingredients together in a salad bowl.

2   Whisk dressing ingredients together and drizzle over salad. Sprinkle with sesame seeds to serve.

Serves 4-6

GROUND PEANUT SOBA NOODLE SALAD

If you cannot acquire soba noodles, any other type of noodle would make an absolutely fine substitute.

300 g fresh soba noodles

2 cups peanuts, roasted

3 tblsp chopped fresh coriander

Dressing:

3 cm piece fresh ginger, grated

4 cloves garlic, crushed

1 red chilli, finely chopped

4 tblsp soya sauce

3 tblsp peanut oil

¼ cup coconut cream

1   Cook noodles in gently boiling water for 3-4 minutes or according to packet instructions. Drain and cool.

2   Reserve ½ cup peanuts. Grind up remaining peanuts in a food processor to resemble breadcrumbs. Add dressing ingredients and blend together.

3   Mix noodles with ground peanut dressing. Garnish with reserved roasted peanuts and chopped coriander.

Serves 6

A CONGLOMERATION OF THE MOST INTERESTING AND SUBTLE FLAVOURS

Spinach, Seaweed and Pickled Ginger Salad

V. Good

ROAST RED PEPPER and ASPARAGUS PENNE with a POPPY-SEED DRESSING

Dips make a great topping for pasta salads, adding extra vibrancy and lip-smacking flavour.

2 red peppers, cut into chunks

1 bunch asparagus, trimmed and halved

½ cup quality black olives

¼ cup fresh sage leaves

olive oil

sea salt

300 g penne or other pasta

Poppy-seed dressing:

3 cloves garlic, crushed

3 tblsp white wine vinegar   *or BALSAMIC vin.*

¼ cup extra virgin olive oil

2 tblsp black poppy seeds

sea salt

freshly ground black pepper

1   Preheat oven to 200ºC. Place peppers, asparagus, olives and sage into a roasting pan. Toss vegetables well in olive oil, sprinkle with salt and roast for 10-15 minutes, turning once during cooking. Remove to cool.

2   Meanwhile, cook the pasta in boiling water until just tender. Drain and set aside to cool.

3   Whisk together dressing ingredients and season well with salt and pepper.

4   Toss pasta in dressing to coat evenly. Mix through prepared roast vegetables.

5   Red pesto (see page 21) makes a delicious topping to this salad.

Serves 6

STIR-FRY CABBAGE SALAD

It may seem odd to serve a stir-fry cold but this really works to produce a green salad that everyone enjoys.

¼ cup peanut oil

½ green cabbage, shredded

2 stalks celery, finely sliced

3 spring onions, sliced

½ cup crunchy sprouts

3 tblsp sesame oil

3 tblsp black or white sesame seeds

1   Heat a wok or large frying pan. Add a little peanut oil and stir-fry cabbage in batches. Stir-fry celery and spring onions. Set vegetables aside to cool.

2   Once cold, mix with sprouts, sesame oil and seeds. Season with salt and pepper to taste.

Serves 4

DIPS MAKE A GREAT TOPPING FOR PASTA SALADS,
ADDING EXTRA VIBRANCY AND LIP-SMACKING FLAVOUR

Roast Red Pepper and Asparagus Penne with a Poppy-Seed Dressing

Chickpea Chilli
Yoghurt Salad

CHICKPEA CHILLI YOGHURT SALAD

Be sure not to add salt to the water when cooking chickpeas or any pulses because they will become tough. Chickpeas, though, definitely benefit from a variety of strong flavours added after cooking to complete the dish.

1½ cups dried chickpeas

1½ cups thick plain yoghurt

2 red chillies, finely chopped

1 tsp Tabasco sauce

finely grated zest and juice of 1 lemon

3 tblsp chopped fresh coriander

3 tblsp chopped fresh dill

3 tblsp chopped fresh mint

1 tblsp celery seeds

2 spring onions, finely chopped

sea salt

freshly ground black pepper

1 Soak chickpeas overnight in plenty of cold water.

2 Next day, drain chickpeas, place in a saucepan and cover with fresh cold water. Bring to the boil then simmer for 1 hour until chickpeas are very tender. Drain well and set aside to cool.

3 Mix remaining salad ingredients together. Toss cold chickpeas in dressing. Chill well to serve.

Serves 6

FENNEL and ROCKET SALAD

A long-time European favourite, fennel bulb is gaining popularity here and this particularly delicious rendition may win over an even greater following. I have demonstrated the making of this interesting dish at Catherine Bell's inspiring Epicurean Workshop cooking school.

1.5 kg fennel bulbs

2 cups dry white wine

1 tblsp olive oil

juice of 2 lemons

2 tblsp sugar

1 tsp sea salt

1 cinnamon stick

3 bay leaves

1–2 cups baby rocket leaves

1 Trim the fennel bulbs. Slice in half and then cut into thin segments.

2 Place all ingredients except rocket into a large pan. Cover and bring to the boil then cook uncovered at a steady simmer until fennel is tender and liquid has almost totally evaporated.

3 Remove to a bowl and allow to cool completely. Remove the cinnamon stick and bay leaves. Add rocket leaves and toss well to combine.

Serves 8

SWEET POTATO ROASTED with LEMON, RED ONIONS and SPICES

Any other root vegetable could be substituted for the sweet potatoes.

4 medium kumara (sweet potatoes), peeled

2 lemons, cut into wedges

2 red onions, peeled and cut into wedges

12 whole cloves garlic, unpeeled

4 bay leaves

1 tsp paprika

½ tsp chilli powder

1 tsp fresh or dried chopped thyme

1 tblsp wholegrain mustard

4 tblsp olive oil

sea salt

freshly ground black pepper

1   Preheat oven to 200ºC.

2   Cut kumara into small, even-sized wedges and parboil for 2 minutes. Drain well. Place kumara, lemons, onions, whole garlic cloves and bay leaves in a roasting pan. Mix remaining ingredients together and pour over vegetables. Toss well to coat.

3   Roast for 20-30 minutes until kumara is tender and golden brown. Serve hot as a vegetable or cold as a salad.

Serves 6

BEAN, WITLOF, BLUE CHEESE and PECAN SALAD

Witlof, known as endive or chicory in some countries, has elegant pale green to white boat-shaped leaves and an ever-so-slightly bitter crunch in flavour. Amazingly, there is now also a red variety of witlof, which would add another colour dimension to this salad.

1 bunch round green beans, trimmed

2 heads witlof, separated

150 g crumbly blue cheese

½ cup pecan nuts, toasted

2 tblsp sherry vinegar

4 tblsp quality walnut oil

sea salt

freshly ground black pepper

1   Blanch beans in boiling salted water until just tender. Drain and plunge into ice-cold water to cool. Drain and dry.

2   Mix salad ingredients together in a bowl. Drizzle with sherry vinegar and walnut oil, and season with salt and pepper to taste.

Serves 4

Sweet Potato Roasted with
Lemon, Red Onions and Spices

EXPERIMENT WITH OTHER STUFFING INGREDIENTS
USING WHATEVER YOU HAVE ON HAND

Stuffed Monkfish in Bacon with Artichokes and Capers

<u>6</u> FISH

Simple and quick cooking methods are really the only way to treat fish with respect. There is nothing more seductive to the palate than fresh fish perfectly cooked. The flesh is soft and pliant, the succulent natural juices intoxicating.

STUFFED MONKFISH in BACON with ARTICHOKES and CAPERS

Monkfish has very white, solid flesh and a smooth flavour. Blue cod or even tuna would also work in this recipe, which needs a firm-textured fish to hold together well. Experiment with other stuffing ingredients using whatever you have on hand or think will combine successfully.

800 g monkfish fillet

1 roasted red pepper, skin removed

8 large basil leaves

2 tomatoes, quartered and seeds removed

sea salt

freshly ground black pepper

4 thin slices bacon, rind removed (or proscuitto)

olive oil

¼ cup capers

½ cup prepared artichoke hearts, in quarters

½ cup dry white wine

1 cup fish or chicken stock

1   Heat oven to 200ºC.

2   Divide fish into 8 even portions. Lay out 4 portions and cover with ¼ pepper, 2 basil leaves and 2 pieces of tomato. Season with salt and pepper and cover with remaining 4 portions of fish. Wrap each in bacon to form secure parcels.

3   Place parcels into an oven pan, drizzle with a little oil and roast for 10 minutes until just cooked. Remove fish and keep warm.

4   Add capers and artichokes to the pan and fry briefly. Add wine, stirring and scraping the bottom of the pan to release cooking juices. Add stock and boil to reduce and thicken. Season with salt and pepper to taste. Slice fish parcels in half and pour sauce over to serve.

Serves 4

BABY OCTOPUS with RED WINE and OLIVES

Baby octopus soak up the red wine's essence with gusto during their gentle cooking. Their great texture and subtle taste is complimented by the addition of olives and rocket to this simple dish.

2 kg baby octopus, cleaned

4 cloves garlic, peeled and crushed

2 bay leaves

1½ cups dry red wine

2 tblsp brown sugar

¼ cup olive oil

2 tblsp sherry or red wine vinegar

½ cup quality black olives

2 lemons, cut into wedges

1 small red onion, very finely diced

3 tblsp chopped fresh parsley

sea salt

freshly ground black pepper

good bunch baby rocket or salad
   leaves

1   Place the octopus, garlic, bay leaves, wine and sugar into a saucepan. Cover and simmer very gently for 20 minutes. Drain octopus, discarding wine and bay leaves.

2   Mix together oil, vinegar, olives, lemon wedges, onion, and parsley. Pour over octopus and toss well to combine. Season with salt and pepper to taste.

3   Serve at room temperature on a bed of rocket.

Serves 4

CELERY SALT and SPICE CRUSTED SALMON

Green olive cream melts beautifully into this spicy salmon. Leaving the skin on salmon keeps it moist and results in a delicious and very edible crispy crust.

1 side fresh salmon with skin on
   (approx. 1 kg)

1 tsp ground cumin

1 tsp ground coriander

1 tsp celery salt (half salt and half
   celery seeds ground together)

pinch cayenne pepper

olive oil

1   Prepare salmon by removing pin bones (you will need a special pair of clean tweezers for this) and cutting into 6 portions. Mix spices together. Brush salmon with a little olive oil then rub with spice mixture.

2   Heat a non-stick pan, add a little olive oil, place salmon pieces skin side down in pan and sear quickly for about 2 minutes on each side. Salmon is best left with a rare centre portion so that it remains succulent.

3   Serve hot. Do try this with dollops of green olive cream (see page 22).

Serves 6

GREAT TEXTURE AND
SUBTLE TASTE

Baby Octopus with Red Wine
and Olives

SEAFOOD LAKSA

This is really a soup but often ends up being a meal in itself. The list of ingredients may seem daunting but don't be put off because most of these are combined to become the basic laksa spice paste. After preparing this, assembling the dish is very easy. Make extra paste as it keeps well in the fridge.

Laksa spice paste:

1 tblsp shrimp paste

2 cloves garlic, chopped

2 cm piece fresh galangal or ginger, chopped

1–2 green chillies

1 kaffir lime leaf, chopped (optional)

2 stalks lemongrass, peeled and chopped

2 tblsp cashew nuts

1 tblsp palm or brown sugar

1 tsp ground turmeric

1 tsp ground coriander

juice of 2 limes

2 tblsp cold water

Soup:

4 tblsp vegetable oil

4 cups quality fish, vegetable or chicken stock

400 ml can coconut milk

12 peeled green prawns

400 g white fish, cubed

1 cup bean sprouts

200 g egg noodles, just cooked

Topping:

¼ telegraph cucumber, seeds removed, finely diced

2 spring onions, finely sliced

2 tblsp chopped fresh coriander

extra finely sliced red chilli to serve

extra limes to serve

1   Grind all spice paste ingredients together with a mortar and pestle or in a food processor to form a smooth paste.

2   Heat a large heavy-based saucepan. Fry spice paste in oil for 5 minutes so that flavours are released. Add stock and bring to the boil then simmer for 15 minutes. Add coconut milk and simmer for a further 5 minutes. Add seafood and simmer for 3 minutes.

3   Add sprouts and pre-cooked noodles to heat through. Ladle into bowls and garnish with cucumber, spring onions and coriander. Serve with lime wedges and extra chilli on the side.

Serves 4

THE LIST OF INGREDIENTS MAY SEEM
DAUNTING BUT DON'T BE PUT OFF

Seafood Laksa

GRILLED MARLIN STEAKS with TAMARIND and CHILLI

The flesh of marlin is wonderfully dense, gelatinous and almost meaty in texture. Tuna or kingfish would make excellent substitutes if necessary.

800 g marlin steaks

1 tblsp vegetable oil

1 red chilli, finely sliced

2 cloves garlic, chopped

3 tblsp palm or brown sugar

¼ cup tamarind concentrate

3 tblsp fish sauce

¼–½ cup water

¼ cup chopped fresh coriander
     leaves

1   Brush marlin steaks with a little oil and cook under a preheated grill, on a barbecue or char-grill pan for about 2 minutes on each side depending on thickness. Fish should be underdone in centre to remain moist.

2   Meanwhile, heat the oil in a small pan, add the chilli and garlic and fry gently for 1 minute. Add the sugar and let it dissolve. Add tamarind, fish sauce and ¼ cup water. Bring back to the boil, add coriander and a little more water if sauce is too thick or strong. Immediately pour over fish and serve.

Serves 4

LIME MARINATED FISH SALAD

Salmon is also amazing presented in this fashion or you could try a half-and-half mix of white fish and salmon.

600 g white fish fillets or salmon

½ cup fresh lime juice

2 cloves garlic, chopped

1 small red onion, finely chopped

3 tomatoes, peeled, seeded and
     chopped

½ cup tomato juice

4 tblsp chopped fresh coriander

1 tsp chopped fresh chilli

2 tblsp olive oil

1 tsp sugar

½ tsp salt

zest of 1 lime

½ cup green olives

1   Cut fish fillets into strips 1 cm thick and place in a non-metallic bowl with lime juice. Leave to marinate for 2 hours.

2   Mix through remaining ingredients and serve.

Serves 4

7 MEAT

It is a wise person who cultivates a good butcher. Support them with your patronage and they will give you in return not only good cuts of meat but invaluable advice, tips and often recipes, and good old-fashioned service. Ask your friendly butcher to cut and bone meats to your cooking requirements; their expertise and knife skills are at your disposal. If you are a little unsure or have questions about, say, which cooking methods suit a certain cut of meat, they are only too happy to share such information.

GLAZED HAM WITH PICKLED FIGS

Ham is an obvious choice when catering for a crowd. A whole glazed ham is a sight to behold, its carving grabs the attention of guests, and that's all before they even taste its wealth of flavour!

1 whole smoked ham cooked on the bone

1 cup white wine

Glaze:

4 tblsp marmalade

3 tblsp honey

5 tblsp brown sugar

2 tblsp wholegrain mustard

¼ tsp ground cloves

1   Preheat oven to 180ºC. Remove skin from ham and score fat. Place in a large roasting pan surrounded by the cup of wine.

2   Mix all glaze ingredients together and smear all over scored fat. Place into the oven and bake for 1 hour, basting at regular intervals until glaze has caramelised to a golden brown. Serve sliced with pickled figs.

Serves 50

PICKLED FIGS

These figs are a drop-dead gorgeous accompaniment to just about any meat but are especially good with ham.

15 fresh figs

2 tblsp salt

1½ cups spiced vinegar

1½ cups sugar

2 cm piece fresh ginger, sliced

1 cinnamon stick

1 tsp whole cloves

1 tsp whole allspice berries

1   Soak figs overnight covered in water mixed with salt. Drain well.

2   Place vinegar, sugar and spices into a saucepan. Bring to the boil, stirring until sugar dissolves.

3   Add figs and simmer very slowly for 30 minutes. Leave figs to cool in liquid.

4   Remove figs and boil liquid to reduce to a thick syrup. Cover figs with syrup and store in the refrigerator.

Makes 15

POMEGRANATE MOLASSES HAS A VIVID ASTRINGENT FLAVOUR AND ADDS A PIQUANT RICHNESS

Lamb Racks with Red Onions and Pomegranate Molasses

LAMB RACKS with RED ONIONS and POMEGRANATE MOLASSES

Pomegranate molasses is a thick, dark syrup that has a vivid astringent flavour and adds a piquant richness to dressings and marinades. It is available from specialist food stores. While not in the least the same, a mixture of lemon juice and molasses could be used as a substitute.

2 whole lamb racks, trimmed

¼ cup pomegranate molasses

½ cup red wine

3 tblsp olive oil

6 small red onions, peeled

2 bay leaves

sea salt

freshly ground black pepper

1 tblsp chopped fresh parsley

1 tblsp chopped fresh mint

1   Place lamb racks into a non-metallic dish. Mix together pomegranate molasses, wine and oil and smear over lamb. Leave to marinate for 4 hours or overnight.

2   Preheat oven to 200ºC. Slice onions into wedges. Place lamb racks into a roasting pan and surround with onions and bay leaves, which have been tossed in the marinade. Season with salt and pepper and roast for 15-20 minutes until lamb is done to your liking. Keep warm while resting for 10 minutes.

3   Slice lamb racks allowing half a rack per person. Serve with onions dusted with herbs and the juices from the pan.

Serves 4

MARMALADE AND SOYA GLAZED SPARE RIBS

The tang of citrus combines with salty soya sauce in this lip-smacking glaze.

½ cup orange or grapefruit marmalade

1½ cups orange juice

½ cup dark soya sauce

3 tblsp lemon juice

3 tblsp brown sugar

½ tsp cayenne pepper

salt and pepper

1.5 kg pork spare ribs

1   Heat all ingredients (except pork), stirring to blend, cool. Pour cold mixture over pork and leave to marinate overnight in a non-metallic bowl.

2   Preheat oven to 190ºC. Place ribs and marinade into a roasting pan and cover with foil. Cook for 2 hours, basting occasionally. Remove covering and cook for 15 minutes longer. Reduce sauce if necessary and pour over ribs to serve.

Serves 4

BEEF and CHORIZO PIES

These are pies filled with robust flavours and covered in a light, almost dumpling-like pastry.

Pastry:

50 g butter

2 cups flour

3 tsp baking powder

1 tsp salt

1 cup milk

Filling:

¼ cup olive oil

1 kg braising beef steak, trimmed

3 chorizo or spicy sausages, sliced

2 onions, peeled and sliced

2 cloves garlic, peeled and crushed

5 tblsp flour

1 cup dry red wine

3 cups beef stock

3 tblsp tomato paste

1 tblsp chopped thyme

sea salt

freshly ground black pepper

1 beaten egg to glaze

1. Rub butter into flour by hand or place flour, baking powder and salt into the bowl of a food processor and pulse to sift. Add butter and process until crumbly.
2. Carefully add milk to bring together to form a smooth dough.
3. Wrap and refrigerate for half an hour before using.

Filling:

1. Brown the meat and chorizo in batches in a hot pan with some oil. Remove to one side. Add remaining oil, onions and garlic and stir over medium heat until beginning to brown. Stir in flour and cook for 1 minute. Remove from the heat and stir in combined wine and stock to form a smooth liquid. Return to the heat and boil until mixture thickens. Stir in tomato paste and thyme. Add meat and chorizo. Simmer very slowly for 45 minutes. Season with salt and pepper and remove to cool.
2. Spoon into 8 1-cup capacity individual pie dishes or ramekins.
3. Roll out pastry to 3 mm thick, cut out 8 pieces and cover pies to form secure lids. Chill for 20 minutes.
4. Heat oven to 180ºC. Glaze pastry with beaten egg. Bake for 20-25 minutes until pastry is golden brown. Serve immediately.

Serves 8

FULL OF ROBUST
FLAVOURS

Beef and Chorizo Pies

FINDING THE REAL THING IS VERY IMPORTANT
TO BUILDING THE RICH LAYERS OF FLAVOUR

Spanish Pork Salad

SPANISH PORK SALAD

If you haven't tried the pronounced flavour of Spanish smoked pimenton then you haven't truly lived! Finding the real thing is very important to building the rich layers of flavour in this salad.

600 g premium quality pork fillets

2 cups baby spinach leaves

½ cup small Spanish olives

Dressing:

3 cloves garlic, crushed

1 tsp Spanish smoked sweet paprika

1 small chilli, finely chopped

½ cup pitted and chopped good quality black olives

juice and finely grated zest of 2 oranges

1 tsp sugar

3 tblsp sherry vinegar

¼ cup extra virgin olive oil

sea salt

freshly ground black pepper

1   Sear pork fillet then roast in an oven heated to 200ºC for 10-15 minutes or until pork is done to your liking. Remove and set aside to cool then slice thinly.

2   Prepare dressing by placing garlic, paprika, chilli and pitted olives into the bowl of a food processor. Process well to combine. Add orange juice and zest (save some zest for garnish), sugar and sherry vinegar, then with the motor running drizzle in olive oil. Season with salt and pepper to taste.

3   Mix pork, spinach and olives together and toss in dressing. Serve garnished with extra orange zest.

Serves 4

ITALIAN SAUSAGES

Working with sausage casings can be a bit of a palaver to the uninitiated so this method of preparation is an easy way out of using casings while still producing excellent sausages.

1 kg pork mince

3 cloves garlic, crushed

1 red chilli, finely chopped

1 tblsp fennel seeds, toasted

½ cup pinenuts, toasted

½ cup grated Parmesan

sea salt

freshly ground black pepper

1   Mix all ingredients together well. Season with salt and pepper.

2   Test for seasoning by cooking a very small amount in a pan. Adjust seasoning if necessary.

3   Divide mixture into 6 and spoon onto 6 pieces of plastic wrap. Form mixture into sausage shapes then roll up and wrap well in plastic wrap, twisting ends firmly to seal. Wrap each parcel securely in foil.

4   Heat water in a large saucepan. Add sausages and poach for 5 minutes. Remove to cool.

5   Unwrap sausages and grill or fry to brown and cook.

Serves 6

SALSAS ARE A CLEVER ALLY FOR SIMPLY PREPARED MEATS

Jamaican Rum Baked Chicken with Salsa

8 POULTRY

White meats are always a popular order in cafés and especially now that they are perceived to be more healthy than other types of meat. Turkey may soon join chicken as an everyday meat because turkey pieces are often available in supermarkets so you don't have to commit to a whole big bird. In any of these dishes, turkey could be substituted for chicken; just remember to make a corresponding adjustment to the cooking time.

JAMAICAN RUM BAKED CHICKEN
with SALSA

Salsas are a clever ally for simply prepared meats; to combine them adds multidimensional tastes and textures.

4 chicken breasts, skin removed

½ cup dark rum

juice of 4 limes

1 tblsp vegetable oil

1 tblsp brown sugar

2 limes, sliced

sea salt

freshly ground black pepper

Chilli banana salsa:

2 bananas, diced

½ red pepper, finely diced

2 red chillies, finely chopped

2 tblsp chopped coriander leaves

1 tblsp brown sugar

½ tsp salt

juice of 3 limes

1 tblsp vegetable oil

1 Place chicken into a non-metallic bowl. Mix rum, lime juice, oil and sugar together, pour over chicken, cover and leave to marinate in the fridge for at least 4 hours, preferably overnight.

2 Preheat oven to 180ºC. Place chicken pieces into a baking dish, top with lime slices, and season with salt and pepper. Bake for 20-30 minutes, basting during cooking until just cooked through. Serve sliced on top of salsa.

Chilli banana salsa:

1 Place all ingredients into a bowl and toss well to combine.

Serves 4

THAI CHICKEN MEATBALLS with FLAT RICE NOODLES

Rice noodles hold such lightness and are very easy to eat, especially topped with these moist and dramatically flavoured chicken meatballs.

1 kg chicken breast, minced

1 cup fresh breadcrumbs

3 cloves garlic, crushed

3 spring onions, finely chopped

½ cup chopped fresh coriander

3 tblsp sweet chilli sauce

juice of 1 lemon

1 egg white

½ tsp salt

vegetable oil for frying

300 g dried flat rice noodles

¼ cup sweet chilli sauce

¼ cup lime juice

1 tblsp fish sauce

3 tblsp peanut oil

¼ cup chopped fresh coriander

1   Mix first 9 ingredients together and shape with damp hands into walnut-sized balls.

2   Heat a large frying pan, add a little oil and gently fry meatballs until browned all over and cooked through.

3   Meanwhile, cook rice noodles for 3 minutes in boiling salted water or according to packet instructions. Drain and toss in chilli sauce, lime juice, fish sauce, peanut oil and coriander mixed together.

4   Serve chicken meatballs on top of noodles.

Serves 6

FRENCH CHICKEN and MUSTARD PIE

Use well-flavoured wholegrain mustard for the best flavour injection.

2 large onions, finely diced

3 tblsp olive oil

4 large chicken breasts, skin removed

4 tblsp wholegrain mustard

¼ cup cream

sea salt

freshly ground black pepper

400 g puff pastry

1 egg yolk to glaze

1   In a large frying pan sweat onions in oil until softened. Cut chicken into large dice and add to pan. Stir-fry for 5 minutes to lightly brown chicken. Stir in mustard and cream and season with salt and pepper. Refrigerate to cool.

2   Roll out just over half the pastry to 3 mm thick and use to line a shallow 24 cm tart tin. Fill with cold chicken mixture. Roll out remaining pastry to cover pie securely as a lid. Chill for 30 minutes. Glaze with egg yolk and bake in an oven heated to 180ºC for 45 minutes until pastry is golden brown.

Serves 8

DRAMATICALLY
FLAVOURED

Thai Chicken Meatballs with
Flat Rice Noodles

Green Pea and Herb
Stuffed Chicken

GREEN PEA and HERB STUFFED CHICKEN

Get your friendly butcher to bone out the chicken if you don't want to attempt
this yourself.

1 whole chicken, boned out

300 g sliced bacon, rind removed

Pea stuffing:

4 cloves garlic

½ cup parsley

¼ cup basil leaves

2 cups peas (fresh or frozen)

2 cups fresh white breadcrumbs

1 small egg, lightly beaten

salt and pepper

1. Lay out the chicken skin-side down and batter to even out meat distribution.

2. In a food processor, purée garlic, parsley, basil and peas. Stir in breadcrumbs and a little egg to bind. Season with salt and pepper to taste. Place stuffing along chicken lengthways. Roll up and wrap in bacon to secure. Place in pan.

3. Roast in an oven heated to 180°C for 1 hour or until cooked by testing that juices run clear. Rest for 10 minutes before slicing.

Serves 8-10

APPLE CIDER CHICKEN with SAGE

Thigh meat is used in this recipe because it has so much more flavour than breast meat.

8 large boneless chicken thighs

5 cloves garlic, chopped

small bunch fresh sage leaves

1 tblsp olive oil

1 tblsp balsamic vinegar

1½ cups apple cider

½ cup chicken stock

sea salt

freshly ground black pepper

¼ cup brown sugar

3 apples, cored and sliced into thin wedges

extra oil to fry apples

1. Place chicken in a non-metallic dish. Cover with garlic, sage leaves, olive oil, balsamic vinegar and apple cider. Leave to marinate overnight.

2. Heat oven to 180°C. Transfer chicken and marinade to a roasting pan. Add stock, salt and pepper to season and sprinkle with brown sugar. Bake for 30 minutes. Meanwhile, fry apple slices in a pan with a little oil until golden brown.

3. Remove chicken from juices and keep warm with apples. Reduce juices until syrupy. Adjust seasoning if necessary. Pour over chicken and apples and serve immediately.

Serves 4

WARM TURKEY SALAD with PINENUTS, PROSCIUTTO and MUSCATELS

Ruth Pretty is an outstanding caterer and this is one of her delicious recipes. I first met Ruth when I was the caterer at a function and she appeared in the kitchen to see who was producing the food. People in the trade can't help themselves, they have to check out the kitchen. I'm glad she did because we are now firm friends. I have made several visits to her fabulous cooking school and catering facility in Te Horo near Wellington to check out her kitchen and I am very impressed, Ruth!

800 g–1 kg turkey tenderloins

olive oil for cooking

grated zest and juice of 1 orange

60 g finely sliced prosciutto, cut into strips

¼ cup pinenuts, toasted

½ cup muscatels, plumped in hot water

¼ cup muscat or port

3 tblsp chopped Italian parsley

2 spring onions, chopped

salad greens for garnish

Dressing:

1 tblsp balsamic vinegar

¼ cup extra virgin olive oil

1 tsp Dijon mustard

sea salt

freshly ground black pepper

1   Preheat oven to 200ºC. Spray or brush turkey with olive oil and place in a roasting pan. Roast for 10 minutes or until juices run clear. Remove from oven to rest.

2   Shred turkey and place in a bowl with remaining salad ingredients.

3   Whisk dressing ingredients together to combine and pour over salad. Toss well to coat and adjust seasoning if necessary.

4   Serve garnished with salad greens.

Serves 8

9 GRAINS AND PULSES

Versatile, fragrant and nourishing, grains and pulses are not only cheap and cheerful but also incredibly interesting to cook with. The things you can do with them are infinitely variable and they add so much to salads, soups and meat dishes. People may have once avoided them because of hippie vegetarian connotations but these dried goodies are a long-respected food source and deservedly so.

CRACKED WHEAT with VEGETABLES and CARAMELISED BAKED FETA

Cracked wheat, also known as bulgur or burghul wheat, is a fantastic staple base ingredient for salads, soups, meat and vegetable dishes. It is totally delicious hot or cold and has a nutty taste that really compliments the vegetables and salty caramelised feta in this dish.

1 cup coarse-grain cracked wheat

1 cup boiling water

juice of 2 lemons

¼ cup olive oil

1 red onion, peeled and diced

3 courgettes, trimmed and thickly sliced

2 red peppers, seeds removed, thickly sliced

2 red chillies, finely chopped

½ cup quality black olives

3 tblsp chopped fresh mint

3 tblsp chopped fresh coriander

sea salt

freshly ground black pepper

Caramelised baked feta:

500 g feta cheese

olive oil

sprigs of fresh rosemary

1   Place cracked wheat into a bowl, pour over boiling water and lemon juice, cover with plastic wrap and leave to steam for 20 minutes.

2   Meanwhile, in a large frying pan stir-fry prepared vegetables in oil until lightly browned. Add olives and herbs and season with salt and pepper to taste.

3   Add softened cracked wheat and toss well to heat through. Adjust seasoning if necessary. Serve topped with caramelised baked feta.

Caramelised baked feta:

1   Heat oven to 200ºC. Break up feta and place into a small ovenproof dish. Drizzle with olive oil and scatter with sprigs of rosemary. Bake for 10–15 minutes until golden brown.

Serves 4

GREEN VEGETABLE RISOTTO

A vibrant green risotto made using a brilliant and easy non-stir method, which I discovered at Sabato in Auckland. Jacqui and Phillip Dixon of Sabato are purveyors of superlative European ingredients and foodstuffs and have become my trusted suppliers and valued friends.

4 cups quality chicken stock

extra virgin olive oil

1 onion, finely diced

3 cloves garlic, crushed

2 cups Italian risotto rice

½ cup dry white wine

sea salt

freshly grated black pepper

grated fresh Parmigiano Reggiano
    (Parmesan)

a little extra stock

2 tblsp butter

Green vegetable flavouring:

3 tblsp extra virgin olive oil

1 small bunch spinach

2 cups peas (fresh or frozen)

1 bunch asparagus, trimmed and
    halved

1 First prepare the flavourings. Heat a frying pan, add oil, spinach and peas and cook, stirring constantly, for 2 minutes. Purée in a blender or food processor, adding a little extra stock if necessary to blend. Blanch asparagus in boiling salted water for 1 minute. Drain and plunge into ice-cold water to cool. Set vegetable flavourings to one side.

2 Heat stock in a saucepan.

3 Heat a heavy-based saucepan or risotto pan. Add a little oil then onion and garlic and sweat over a medium heat. Add risotto rice and allow to toast but not brown, stirring continuously for 2 minutes. Add wine and allow to evaporate.

4 Add hot stock all at once and a little salt and pepper. Bring to the boil, stir, then cover and simmer for 15 minutes.

5 Stir in prepared flavouring then allow to rest, covered, for a few minutes.

6 Stir through Parmigiano, a little extra hot stock and butter to create a creamy consistency.

Serves 6

MADE USING A BRILLIANT AND
EASY NON-STIR METHOD

Green Vegetable Risotto

PARTICULARLY GOOD SERVED WITH A
FAVOURITE CHUTNEY AND A LIGHT SALAD

Couscous Fritters

COUSCOUS FRITTERS

Fritters are always incredibly popular café fare. They make a great light lunch and are particularly good served with a favourite chutney and a light salad.

1 cup couscous

1 cup boiling water

3 tblsp oil

1 onion, finely chopped

1 red pepper, finely diced

3 tblsp chopped fresh basil

½ cup capers

¼ cup plain natural yoghurt

1 egg, lightly beaten

salt and pepper

oil for shallow frying

1 Pour boiling water over couscous, stir, cover with plastic wrap and set aside for 10 minutes.

2 Heat a pan, add oil, onion and red pepper and cook until soft.

3 Fluff up couscous grains with a fork. Mix onion, basil, yoghurt and egg into couscous. Season well with salt and pepper. Using damp hands form mixture into fritters.

4 Shallow fry over medium heat for a couple of minutes on each side until golden. Drain on paper towels.

Makes 12

PUMPKIN CORNBREAD CAKE

This is a great medium to mop up juices of meat or vegetable ragouts.

1½ cups fine cornmeal

1 cup plain flour

2 tsp baking powder

½ tsp baking soda

½ tsp salt

1 cup grated Cheddar cheese

3 spring onions, finely sliced

2 tblsp chopped fresh oregano

1 cup cooked, mashed pumpkin

1 cup plain yoghurt

2 eggs, lightly beaten

¼ cup olive oil

¼ cup extra grated Cheddar cheese

1 Preheat oven to 180ºC. Grease a 22 cm spring-form cake tin and dust with a little cornmeal.

2 Combine cornmeal, flour, baking powder and soda, salt, cheese, spring onion and oregano in a large bowl.

3 Mix together pumpkin, yoghurt, eggs and oil. Pour pumpkin mixture over dry ingredients and stir to combine. Pour into prepared cake tin and scatter over extra cheese. Bake for 45 minutes until a skewer inserted comes out clean.

4 Serve sliced with juicy meat or vegetable dishes.

Serves 8

BUTTERED QUINOA with SPICY BLACK BEANS

Quinoa, pronounced keen-wah, an ancient Incan staple, is one of the oldest grains on earth. Most quinoa comes from South America and is readily available in health food shops. Quinoa is one of the best grain-based sources of protein, calcium and iron. This nutritional wonder grain cooks quickly and gives texture and crunch to salads, soups and baked dishes.

Buttered quinoa:

1 cup quinoa

2 cups vegetable or chicken stock

100 g butter

sea salt

freshly ground black pepper

Spicy black beans:

1 cup black turtle beans

2 tblsp vegetable oil

1 tsp ground coriander

½ tsp chilli powder

3 cloves garlic, crushed

1 red onion, finely diced

1 red pepper, seeds removed, finely diced

1 cup sweetcorn kernels (fresh or frozen)

2 cups vegetable or chicken stock

400 g can peeled tomatoes, chopped

juice of 2 limes

½ cup chopped fresh coriander leaves

sea salt

freshly ground black pepper

1 Rinse the quinoa for 2 minutes to remove natural bitter coating.

2 Bring stock to the boil in a saucepan. Stir in quinoa and simmer uncovered for 20 minutes, or until translucent and the liquid is absorbed. Stir in the butter so that it melts. Season with salt and pepper.

Spicy black beans:

1 Soak beans overnight in cold water. Next day, drain beans and place in a saucepan. Cover with fresh cold water and bring to the boil. Simmer for 1 hour until beans are tender. Drain.

2 Meanwhile, heat oil in a large pan. Add spices, garlic and onion and cook gently for 10 minutes to soften onion. Add vegetables, stock and tomatoes and bring to the boil then simmer for 15 minutes. Add the beans to reheat.

3 Stir in lime juice and coriander. Season with salt and pepper to taste.

Serves 6

QUINOA IS ONE OF THE BEST GRAIN-BASED
SOURCES OF PROTEIN, CALCIUM AND IRON

Buttered Quinoa with Spicy Black Beans

ADD LASHINGS TO A CHUNKY HOME-MADE
SANDWICH FOR CRUNCH AND ZING

Zucchini Bread-and-Butter Pickle

<u>10</u> PRESERVES

Preserving, it could be said, is akin to bottling sunlight. All the warmth and flavour of sun-ripened fruit and vegetables can be captured and stored away to be brought out again at a later date when we notice their absence. Usually long after the café has closed for the day I launch into preserving with a passionate heart. At my work's end I gain a feeling of total satisfaction from gazing upon rows of colourfully filled jars. Judging by the increase in purchases of hand-made preserves from the food store, many people don't have the time to bottle these pungent mixtures for themselves. Or maybe they have developed a liking for my recipes, some of which I am only too happy to share with you here.

ZUCCHINI BREAD-AND-BUTTER PICKLE

Perfect with cheese and bread or add lashings to a chunky home-made sandwich for crunch and zing.

10 thin green zucchini

3 large onions

¼ cup salt

6 cups cold water

3 cups white wine vinegar

2 cups sugar

1 tsp turmeric

1 tsp celery seeds

2 tblsp mustard seeds

2 tblsp cornflour

1   Finely slice zucchini and onions. Cover with salt and water, and leave overnight covered with plastic wrap. Next day drain thoroughly.

2   Place remaining ingredients except cornflour into a preserving pan or large saucepan. Bring to the boil, stirring until sugar dissolves. Add cornflour mixed to a smooth paste with a little water and boil for 2 minutes until cornflour cooks and thickens liquid. Add drained vegetables and bring back to the boil for 2 minutes more.

3   Ladle into hot sterilised jars and seal well. Store in a cool, dark place.

Makes about 8 cups

SPICY PLUM CHUTNEY

Half the spice of café eating comes from sampling all the extras served on the side. Chutneys are the best accompaniment to so many savoury café foods.

2 kg dark plums, stoned and
  chopped

500 g onions, peeled and diced

5 cups brown sugar

4 cups malt vinegar

1 tblsp salt

1 tsp chilli powder

1 tsp ground cloves

1 Place all ingredients into a preserving pan or large saucepan. Bring to the boil, stirring until sugar dissolves.

2 Boil very gently, stirring frequently, for about 1½ hours or until chutney is very thick and jam-like.

3 Ladle into hot sterilised jars and seal well.

Makes about 8 cups

TAMARIND CHUTNEY

Tamarind has a fabulous sour flavour and is used in a lot of Indian and Thai recipes. It can be purchased in block form or as a concentrate. Look for dark, glossy pulp as this has a deeper flavour to its pale counterpart.

200 g tamarind pulp

2 cups boiling water

2 cm piece fresh ginger, chopped

2 small chillies, chopped

2 tsp garam masala, toasted

2 cups spiced vinegar

2 cups brown sugar

1 tsp salt

1 Pour boiling water over tamarind seed pulp, mash with a fork and leave to soak for 30 minutes. Strain to remove liquid, which is called tamarind water. Discard seed pulp.

2 Place tamarind water and remaining ingredients into a saucepan. Bring to the boil, stirring until sugar dissolves. Simmer for 15-20 minutes to thicken. Transfer to a blender and purée.

3 Ladle into hot sterilised jars and seal well.

4 Serve as a chutney or thin with water to desired consistency and use as a dipping sauce.

Makes about 6 cups

APRICOT CHUTNEY

A sweetly pungent chutney enhanced with interesting flavours of India. Fenugreek is an ancient herb; the leaves and the seeds of which are much used in Indian cookery. The seeds are a basic ingredient of curry powder, so don't fret if you cannot find the extra seeds for this recipe.

2 kg apricots, stoned and chopped

500 g onions, peeled and chopped

3 cups sugar

1 tblsp salt

2 tblsp hot curry powder

1 tblsp yellow mustard seeds

1 tblsp fenugreek seeds, lightly toasted and ground (optional)

3 cups spiced vinegar

1 Place all ingredients into a preserving pan or large saucepan. Bring to the boil, stirring until sugar dissolves.

2 Boil gently, stirring frequently, for about 1 hour or until chutney is very thick and jam-like.

3 Ladle into hot sterilised jars and seal well.

Makes about 6 cups

CHILLI PEPPER TOMATO RELISH

8 medium tomatoes, peeled and roughly chopped

2 red peppers, seeds removed and diced

1 large onion, peeled and diced

4 cloves garlic, chopped

1 tblsp grated fresh ginger

2 cups cider vinegar

2 cups sugar

5 small red chillies, finely chopped

juice of 2 lemons

1 tsp ground cinnamon

½ tsp ground allspice

2 tsp salt

1 Combine tomatoes with red peppers, onion, garlic and ginger in a large saucepan. Simmer uncovered stirring occasionally for 15 minutes until softened.

2 Add remaining ingredients and bring to the boil, stirring until sugar has dissolved. Simmer for about 1 hour or until mixture is thick and jammy.

3 Ladle into hot sterilised jars and seal well.

Makes about 6 cups

TRIPLE BERRY JAM

This luscious ruby-red conserve is the sum of three favourite berry jams combined.

2 cups raspberries

1 cup blackberries

1 cup hulled and chopped strawberries

juice of 1 lemon

3½ cups sugar

1 Place berries and lemon juice into a preserving pan or large saucepan. Cook slowly over a gentle heat until juices run from berries. Add sugar, stirring until dissolved.

2 Boil briskly for 5-10 minutes or until setting point is reached. Test by placing a spoonful onto a chilled plate. If the sample wrinkles when pushed with a finger, the jam is ready to set.

3 Skim any foam from the surface. Allow to cool for 10 minutes then stir to distribute fruit evenly.

4 Ladle into hot sterilised jars and seal well.

Makes about 5 cups

VANILLA BLACK CHERRY JAM

Vanilla adds a balmy fragrance to this dense cherry jam.

1 kg black cherries, stoned

1 vanilla pod, split to remove seeds

5 cups sugar

juice of 1 lemon

1 Place all ingredients into a preserving pan or large saucepan. Bring to the boil, stirring until sugar has dissolved, then simmer until cherries are just tender.

2 Raise the heat and boil for 5-10 minutes or until setting point is reached (see Triple Berry Jam above).

3 Remove from the heat and skim any foam from the surface. Remove the vanilla pod. Allow to cool for 10 minutes then stir to distribute fruit evenly.

4 Ladle into hot sterilised jars and seal well.

Makes about 6 cups

97

PASSIONFRUIT CURD

The individual flavour of passionfruit really comes through in this curd. Strain the pulp if you don't enjoy the sensation of crunching on pips.

125 g butter

1 cup caster sugar

juice of 2 lemons

3 eggs, lightly beaten

pulp from 4 passionfruit

1   Place butter, sugar and lemon juice into a double boiler or a heat-proof bowl over a saucepan of gently boiling water. Heat until butter has melted and sugar dissolved.

2   Strain beaten eggs to remove any lumps. Pour first mixture onto beaten eggs, whisking well to incorporate.

3   Return mixture to the double boiler. Stir continuously over a gentle heat until mixture thickens to coat the back of a spoon. Do not allow mixture to boil or it will curdle. Remove from the heat and stir in passionfruit pulp.

4   Ladle into hot sterilised jars and seal well. Store in a cool, dark place. Refrigerate after opening.

Makes about 2 cups

ROSE PETAL JAM

This compelling floral syrup with supposed secret powers appears in the story of the Arabian Nights.

200 g perfumed dark red rose petals

2 cups sugar

pectin

juice of 2 lemons

1 litre water

rose water (optional)

1   Roughly chop rose petals and place in a bowl with the sugar. Cover and leave for 24 hours.

2   Next day, place rose petals, sugar, pectin, lemon juice and water into a preserving pan or large saucepan. Bring to the boil, stirring until sugar dissolves, then simmer for 20 minutes.

3   Boil for 5 minutes until setting point is reached (see Triple Berry Jam, page 96). Add rose water to increase flavour if desired.

4   Ladle into hot sterilised jars and seal well.

Makes about 2 cups

TANGELO MARMALADE

Tangelos or tangerines have a very distinctive flavour and make wonderfully rich marmalade.

1 kg tangelos
juice of 2 lemons
1.5 litres water
1 kg sugar

1. Cut the tangelos in half, squeeze out the juice and reserve. Scrape the membranes from the skins and reserve with the pips tied in a clean muslin bag. Cut the peel into fine strips.

2. Place the tangelo and lemon juices, peel, water and muslin bag into a large saucepan or preserving pan. Bring to the boil, then simmer for 1 hour until peel is tender and the mixture is reduced by half.

3. Remove the muslin bag, pressing so that juices flow back into the pan. Discard the bag.

4. Add the sugar and stir until dissolved. Boil hard for 15-20 minutes, stirring occasionally, until setting point is reached (see Triple Berry Jam, page 96). Remove from the heat and skim any foam from the surface. Leave to stand for 10 minutes, then stir and ladle into hot sterilised jars and seal well.

Makes 6-8 cups

BANANA and LIME JAM

Strange but true, a delicious tropical jam.

juice and finely grated zest of 2 limes
juice of 2 lemons
2 cups sugar
4 bananas, sliced

1. Place lemon and lime juice and sugar into a saucepan and bring to the boil, stirring until sugar dissolves. Boil for 2 minutes to form a syrup.

2. Add bananas and lime zest and cook for a further 2 minutes.

3. Store in the refrigerator, as this does not bottle well.

Makes about 3 cups

Pacific Panforte

<u>11</u> SWEETS

It is fascinating how people are attracted to pretty little cakes and desserts like bees to a honey pot. Even those who tell me they are never tempted, are not even interested in anything sweet, have been enticed by some of these little fancies. Slices from whole cakes are a great temptation but distinctive individual mini cakes are particularly appealing to café citizens. The singularity of these creations seems to hold a certain irresistible charm, not to mention their alluring taste.

PACIFIC PANFORTE

Panforte is best appreciated in thin slices both because it is profoundly intense and also because the suspended fruits reflect the light like a stained-glass window.

1 cup macadamia nuts, toasted and roughly chopped

1 cup dried pineapple, cut into chunks

1 cup dried papaya, cut into chunks

1 cup dried mango, cut into chunks

¼ cup honey

½ cup sugar

60 g dark chocolate, chopped

2 tsp vanilla extract

½ cup desiccated coconut threads

⅔ cup plain flour

1 tsp ground cardamom

icing sugar to dust

1 Combine nuts, fruit and cardamom in a mixing bowl.

2 Heat honey and sugar in a saucepan until sugar dissolves. Boil until mixture reaches the soft ball stage, which is when a small amount is dropped into cold water and forms soft, pliant balls. Add chocolate and vanilla and stir until chocolate is melted. Pour onto dry ingredients and quickly mix to combine.

3 Press into a well-greased or rice paper lined 22 cm cake tin with a removable base.

4 Bake in an oven heated to 150ºC for about 1 hour or until set. Remove from tin while still warm.

5 Dust with icing sugar and cut into thin wedges to serve. Store in an airtight container.

Makes one 22 cm panforte

PASTA DE NADA

I thought I'd died and gone to heaven when I first tasted these Portuguese custard tarts on the island of Macau, which has a fantastic Portuguese influence. I have been crazy for them ever since, especially when they are still warm from the oven.

200 g flaky pastry

Filling:
½ cup sugar
½ cup water
2 tblsp cornflour
1 cup milk
2 egg yolks
1 tsp vanilla extract

1   Roll out pastry to 2 mm thick. Cut 12 x 10 cm rounds and fit into patty pans. Lightly prick with a fork and refrigerate until needed.

2   Place sugar and water into a small saucepan. Bring to the boil, stirring until sugar dissolves. Boil for 2 minutes to form a syrup.

3   Mix cornflour to a smooth paste with a little of the measured milk. Whisk milk, cornflour mix, egg yolks, vanilla and sugar syrup together and return to the pan. Stir over a low heat until mixture thickens. Remove to a bowl to cool, covering the surface with plastic wrap.

4   Preheat oven to 200ºC. Spoon mixture evenly into prepared pastry cases. Bake for 20 minutes until custard is lightly browned and set. Transfer to a wire rack to cool.

Makes 12

ANZAC BISCUITS

Australians and New Zealanders will always have a soft spot for these biscuits.

100g butter
1 tblsp golden syrup
1 tsp baking soda
1 tblsp hot water
½ cup sugar
½ cup desiccated coconut
½ cup rolled oats
¼ cup chopped dried apricots
¼ cup sunflower seeds
¾ cup plain flour
pinch salt

1   Melt butter, golden syrup, baking soda and hot water together. Cool, then mix into combined dry ingredients.

2   Heat oven to 180ºC. Place rounded spoonfuls on a greased baking tray. Bake for 15 minutes or until golden. Remove to a rack to cool.

Makes 30

Pasta De Nada

FRAGRANT WITH A DELICATE INFUSION OF ROSES

Persian Rose and Aniseed Cakes

PERSIAN ROSE and ANISEED CAKES

These exotic little cakes are fragrant with a delicate infusion of roses, which creates a beautiful contrast to the musky spice of aniseed.

125 g butter, softened

1¼ cups sugar

4 eggs

¾ cup milk

2 cups plain flour

2 tsp baking powder

¼ cup aniseeds

Rose syrup:

1 cup sugar

1 cup water

½ cup lemon juice

2 tblsp rose water

1   Preheat oven to 160ºC. Grease and flour 12 individual cake or muffin moulds or one 22 cm spring-form cake tin.

2   Cream butter and sugar until pale, then beat in eggs. Stir in milk alternately with sifted dry ingredients and aniseeds. Pour cake mix into prepared tins. Bake small cakes for 20–25 minutes and whole cake for 1 hour 10 minutes or until a skewer inserted comes out clean. Cool a little before removing from tins.

3   Drizzle with rose syrup and decorate with rose petals if desired.

Rose syrup:

1   Place all ingredients into a pan and boil for 5 minutes to form a syrup.

Serves 12

PEAR and POLENTA CAKE

Caramelised pears sit prettily on top of a polenta sponge, which sops up their sticky sweet nectar.

2 tblsp raw sugar

2 pears, cored and sliced

2 large eggs

1¼ cups sugar

⅔ cup olive oil

⅔ cup white wine

1 tsp vanilla extract

1¼ cups flour

1½ tsp baking powder

½ cup instant polenta

Pear syrup:

1 cup sugar

½ cup water

3 pears, cored and sliced

juice and peeled rind of 2 lemons

1 Preheat oven to 160°C. Grease a 22 cm spring-form cake tin. Sprinkle base of tin evenly with raw sugar and arrange sliced pears to cover.

2 Whisk eggs and sugar until pale and very thick. Gently beat in oil, wine and vanilla. Fold in sifted dry ingredients. Pour into prepared cake tin. Bake for 1 hour or until a skewer inserted comes out clean.

3 Allow cake to cool for 5 minutes before inverting onto a serving plate. Pour pear syrup over cake to serve.

Pear syrup:

1 Heat sugar and water in a heavy-based pan until sugar dissolves. Boil until mixture begins to caramelise. Add pears, lemon juice and rind carefully to the pan because the caramel may splatter and hiss. Simmer gently for 5 minutes until pears are just tender.

Serves 10

MANGO and PINEAPPLE CHEESECAKE

This deliciously silky, fruit-filled dessert is best made in advance, both because it needs a good amount of time to set and because the delicate flavours are then given a chance to mingle and intensify.

Base:

200 g digestive biscuits

¼ cup sugar

1 tsp cinnamon

100 g butter, melted

Filling:

½ cup boiling water

1 tblsp powdered gelatine

300 g cream cheese

½ cup sugar

juice of 2 limes or 1 lemon

1¼ cups crushed pineapple and juice

chopped flesh of 1 fresh mango

1¼ cups cream

1   Crush biscuits in a food processor or with a rolling pin. Mix with sugar, cinnamon and melted butter. Spread evenly into the base of a 24 cm spring-form cake tin and press down well. Wrap a paper collar around the inside of the tin to enclose the filling.

2   Sprinkle gelatine over measured boiling water in a small bowl or cup and leave to swell.

3   Beat cream cheese, sugar and lime or lemon juice together until smooth. Mix in pineapple and mango.

4   Heat bowl of gelatine in a water bath or microwave oven for 40 seconds to dissolve. Mix well into filling.

5   Whip cream to stiff peaks and fold into filling. Pour over prepared base and refrigerate for at least 6 hours but preferably overnight to set.

Serves 12

ITALIAN STYLE STRAWBERRY TRIFLE

Packed into little portable containers, trifle also makes a great picnic or take-out dessert.

3 cups strawberries, hulled (reserve
  6 unhulled to garnish)

2 tblsp sugar

¼ cup brandy or liqueur (optional)

200 g trifle sponge

1 vanilla pod

3 egg yolks

¼ cup sugar

300 g mascarpone

1   Purée strawberries with sugar and liqueur if desired. Slice sponge into thin layers and cut out circles to fit serving glasses (a pastry cutter works well).

2   Split the vanilla pod and remove the seeds. Beat egg yolks, sugar and vanilla seeds together in a bowl over simmering water until thick and pale. Remove from heat and beat until cool. Beat in mascarpone.

3   Alternately layer strawberry purée, sponge drizzled with liqueur then mascarpone mix into glasses, finishing with purée. Chill well and serve topped with a whole strawberry.

Serves 6

BLUEBERRY SOUR CREAM CAKE

Blueberries bleed their intensity into this delectable sour cream cake.

125 g butter

¾ cup sugar

finely grated zest of 1 lemon

3 eggs

1 tsp vanilla extract

½ cup sour cream

1 cup plain flour

1 tsp baking powder

1 cup fresh or frozen blueberries

icing sugar to dust

1   Preheat oven to 160ºC. Grease and flour a 22 cm spring-form cake tin.

2   Cream butter and sugar until pale. Beat in zest, eggs, vanilla and sour cream. Fold in sifted dry ingredients. Lastly, gently fold in blueberries. Pour into prepared cake tin. Bake for 1 hour or until a skewer inserted comes out clean.

3   Allow to cool before removing from cake tin.

4   Dust with icing sugar to serve.

Serves 10

TRIFLE ALSO MAKES A GREAT
PICNIC OR TAKE-OUT DESSERT

Italian Style Strawberry Trifle

BANANA and FEIJOA CAKE with LEMON ICING

Although native to South America and once known as 'pineapple guava', the feijoa is now grown essentially in New Zealand. Unusual and intensely flavoured feijoas are even more potent when cooked. If unavailable they can be omitted, resulting in a very nice banana cake, or try adding guavas instead.

250 g butter

1 cup sugar

½ cup brown sugar

3 eggs

2 mashed bananas

5 feijoas, peeled and chopped

1 tsp baking soda

3 tblsp boiling milk

2¼ cups self-raising flour

½ tsp freshly grated nutmeg

Lemon icing:

100 g butter, softened

2 cups icing sugar

juice and finely grated zest of 1
    lemon

1   Preheat oven to 160°C. Grease a 24 cm spring-form cake tin.

2   Cream butter and sugars until pale. Add eggs and bananas and beat well. Gently mix in feijoas and baking soda dissolved in boiling milk.

3   Fold in sifted flour and nutmeg. Pour mixture into prepared cake tin.

4   Bake for 45 minutes or until a skewer inserted comes out clean.

5   Remove from tin once cold and ice with lemon icing.

Lemon icing:

1   Whisk all ingredients together to form a pale fluffy icing. Spread over cake with a spatula.

Serves 10

STICKY FIG KISSES with CARAMEL SAUCE

Sweet figs are held captive by the softness of these irresistible kisses. When figs are not available, try substituting any other fruit of choice.

1 cup golden syrup

½ cup water

75 g butter

½ cup tightly packed brown sugar

2 cups plain flour

2 tsp cinnamon

2 tsp ground ginger

½ tsp ground cloves

½ tsp ground nutmeg

½ tsp salt

1 tsp baking soda

8 fresh figs, cut in half

Caramel sauce:

100 g butter

½ cup cream

1 cup tightly packed brown sugar

1 tsp vanilla extract

1   Preheat oven to 170ºC. Grease 16 muffin pans.

2   Combine golden syrup, water, butter and brown sugar in a saucepan. Heat until butter melts and sugar has dissolved. Remove from the heat and allow to cool completely.

3   Sift dry ingredients together into a mixing bowl. Stir golden syrup mixture into dry ingredients and mix to form a smooth batter.

4   Spoon evenly into prepared muffin pans to fill by three-quarters. Top each with a fig half. Bake for 20 minutes or until cakes spring back when pressed with a fingertip. Serve with caramel sauce.

Makes 16

Caramel sauce:

1   Place all ingredients into a saucepan over a gentle heat until butter melts and sugar has dissolved. Boil for 2 minutes until mixture is syrupy. Sauce can be served hot or cold.

Makes 1¾ cups

Chocolate Cherry
Almond Cakes

CHOCOLATE CHERRY ALMOND CAKES

People who love good food are suspicious of perfection. Only a machine can turn out regular, symmetrical shapes and that is the beauty of hand-made food. Like the cherries on top, these cakes have a character all of their own.

ground almonds for dusting

200 g butter

1 cup caster sugar

4 eggs

2 cups ground almonds

¾ cup chopped dark chocolate (or chocolate chips)

2 tsp vanilla extract

1 tsp cinnamon

1 tsp baking powder

¼ cup plain flour

1 tblsp cocoa powder

1½ cups pitted fresh cherries or 425 g can stoneless black cherries, drained

extra cherries for decoration if desired

1   Preheat oven to 170ºC. Grease 12 individual mini cake moulds or one 22 cm spring-form cake tin and lightly dust with ground almonds.

2   Cream butter and sugar until pale. Add eggs one at a time, beating well between additions. Stir in ground almonds, chopped chocolate and vanilla. Sift together cinnamon, baking powder, flour and cocoa and gently stir into cake mixture. Lastly, fold in drained cherries.

3   Pour into prepared tins. Bake little cakes for 25 minutes or whole cake for 1 hour.

4   Remove from tins once cold. Drizzle with chocolate glaze and garnish with fresh cherries if desired.

Serves 12

CHOCOLATE GLAZE

A glossy, luscious chocolate glaze can be put to many uses. It adorns these little cakes like embroidery but will also form a solid sheet of icing over a large cake or thrill your taste buds as a hot chocolate sauce.

1 cup chopped quality dark chocolate

1 tblsp golden syrup

1 tblsp butter

1 tblsp brandy, rum or whiskey

½ cup hot water

1 Place chocolate in a bowl with golden syrup, butter, brandy, rum or whiskey and hot water. Melt together over a pan of simmering water or in a microwave. Stir gently to form a smooth sauce.

Makes about 1 cup

PRUNE and SULTANA TEA LOAVES

This is a lovely teabread filled with prunes and golden sultanas. Serve it hot or cold spread with a little butter.

1¼ cups hot tea

1 cup chopped prunes

75 g butter

1 cup raw sugar

1 tblsp golden syrup

1 egg

½ tsp vanilla extract

1½ cups self-raising flour

¼ tsp salt

¼ tsp freshly grated nutmeg

½ tsp cinnamon

½ cup sultanas

1   Pour hot tea over prunes and butter. Set aside until cooled to room temperature.

2   Cream sugar and golden syrup with tea, prune and butter mixture, add egg and vanilla and beat well. Stir in sifted flour, salt and spices, and lastly sultanas.

3   Pour into a greased and floured 23 cm loaf tin or 8 individual loaf tins. Bake at 170ºC for 45 minutes or 15 minutes for individual loaves or until a skewer inserted comes out clean.

Makes 1 x 23 cm loaf or 8 individual loaves

FRUIT MINCE and POLENTA SHORTCAKE

Offer this shortcake as an alternative to traditional festive treats or make it all year round if you love fruit mince as much as I do.

1½ cups instant pre-cooked polenta

2½ cups self-raising flour

1½ cups raw sugar

1 tsp baking powder

1 tsp cinnamon

250 g butter, cubed

1 egg, lightly beaten

1½ cups traditional fruit mince

1   Place polenta, flour, sugar, baking powder and cinnamon into the bowl of a food processor and pulse to sift. Add butter and process until crumbly. Add beaten egg and briefly work in to bring mixture together.

2   Spread half the mixture into the bottom of a greased 26 cm cake tin. Cover with fruit mince and then with remaining polenta mixture.

3   Bake in an oven heated to 160ºC for 1 hour.

Serves 12

SERVE IT HOT OR COLD SPREAD
WITH A LITTLE BUTTER

Prune and Sultana Tea Loaves

THIS HAS TO BE TOTALLY IMPOSSIBLE TO RESIST

Very Berry Summer Pudding

VERY BERRY SUMMER PUDDING

A cheery pudding that echoes memories of summers gone by. Brimming with berries and stained with their juices, this has to be totally impossible to resist.

10–12 slices day-old sandwich bread

8 cups fresh or frozen mixed berries — equal quantities of raspberries, blackberries, blueberries and strawberries is a good combination

juice of 1 lemon

1½ cups sugar

1 Line a 6-8 cup capacity bowl with plastic wrap for easy removal.

2 Place all the berries, lemon juice and sugar into a saucepan. Bring to the boil, stirring very gently until sugar has dissolved. Boil for 1 minute then remove to cool completely.

3 Remove crusts from bread and slice into strips. Dip strips into berries to soak up a little juice then line mould completely with overlapping pieces of bread. Spoon berries and juice into mould and cover with remaining strips of bread. Bring up plastic wrap to cover pudding.

4 Place a plate on top and a weight to press the pudding. Refrigerate for 1-2 days to compress.

5 Invert pudding over serving plate and pull edges of plastic wrap to release.

Serves 12

EATING THIS TART GIVES
MELT-IN-YOUR-MOUTH PLEASURE

Deep Lime and Lemon Cream Tart

DEEP LIME and LEMON CREAM TART

Based on a classic Roux brothers' recipe, eating this tart gives melt-in-your-mouth pleasure combined with a zesty citrus tang.

400 g sweet short pastry (below)

Filling:
9 eggs
2 cups sugar
1½ cups cream
zest of 2 lemons and 2 limes
juice of 6 lemons
juice of 6 limes

1   Roll out pastry to 3 mm thick and line a 25 cm deep tart tin. Chill well. Bake blind at 190ºC for 10 minutes. Remove baking beans and return to oven for a further 5 minutes to dry pastry.

Filling:

1   Gently whisk all ingredients together until sugar has dissolved. Pour into pre-baked pastry shell. Lower oven temperature to 150ºC. Bake for 45 minutes or until just set. Allow to cool completely before removing from tin.

Serves 10

SWEET SHORTCRUST PASTRY

This pastry is very forgiving, patches well if necessary, and cooks to a lovely crisp golden crust. To store, wrap well in plastic wrap. Lasts in the refrigerator for up to 1 week or in the deep freeze for up to 3 months.

250 g butter, softened
¾ cup caster sugar
1 egg
3 cups plain flour

1   Beat butter, sugar and egg together to just combine – do not cream mixture. Gently mix in flour to form a dough. Wrap in plastic wrap and refrigerate half an hour or until firm enough to roll out.

2   Use as recipe directs.

Makes 850 g, enough to produce 2–3 sweet tart recipes

APRICOT MACAROONS

These tempting sweet nibbles are perfect with an espresso coffee. An added bonus is that they provide a great way to utilise excess egg whites, which are often on hand in the kitchen.

½ cup egg whites

1¼ cups sugar

1 tblsp honey

1 tsp vanilla extract

2¾ cups fine desiccated coconut

¼ cup plain flour

¾ cup finely chopped dried apricots

1　Heat oven to 160ºC and grease a baking tray.

2　In a bowl set over a pan of simmering water, whisk together egg whites, sugar, honey and vanilla until mixture is very pale and sugar has dissolved (about 5 minutes). Remove from heat and stir in coconut, cocoa and flour sifted together. Chill until firm.

3　Shape into balls and place onto baking tray. Bake for 25 minutes. Remove to cool. Store in an airtight container.

Makes about 36

COFFEE CRUMBLE CAKES

Sweet little coffee cakes with a streusel crumble topping.

2½ cups flour

2½ tsp baking powder

pinch salt

1½ cups brown sugar

2 tsp cinnamon

250 g butter

1 tsp ground coffee beans

¼ cup very strong coffee

¼ cup milk

¼ tsp baking soda

2 eggs, lightly beaten

1　Sift dry ingredients into a bowl. Rub in butter until crumbly. Reserve 1 cup of this mixture for topping, add cinnamon to this and set to one side.

2　Combine coffees, milk and baking soda and add with beaten eggs to dry mix. Stir gently to form a batter. Spoon into greased muffin pans. Sprinkle each with crumble topping.

3　Bake at 170ºC for 25 minutes. Best served warm.

Makes 12

PERFECT WITH AN ESPRESSO COFFEE

Apricot Macaroons

Jam Swirl Biscuits

JAM SWIRL BISCUITS

A buttery biscuit holding spirals of jam – just the thing to have with a good coffee.

150 g butter

¾ cup sugar

1 egg yolk

1 tsp vanilla extract

1 cup plain flour

½ tsp baking powder

pinch salt

3 tblsp plum or berry jam

1   Cream butter and sugar together. Beat in egg yolk and vanilla. Stir in sifted dry ingredients to form a firm dough.

2   Roll out dough to 5 mm thick in the shape of a long rectangle about 15 cm x 35 cm. Spread with jam and roll up tightly into a log. Wrap in plastic wrap and refrigerate until firm.

3   Preheat oven to 180ºC. Lightly grease 2 baking sheets. Cut log into 5 mm slices on the diagonal and place on baking sheets. Bake 10 minutes until golden. Transfer to wire racks to cool.

Makes 20

CHOCOLATE FUDGE CAKE

Many people are addicted to this gooey cake! It can be difficult to cut because it is so fudge-like, so always use a hot wet knife for best results.

1 cup water

250 g butter

250 g dark chocolate

2 cups caster sugar

1½ cups self-raising flour

¼ cup cocoa powder

2 eggs, lightly beaten

1 tsp vanilla extract

Sour chocolate icing:

¾ cup dark chocolate in pieces

½ cup sour cream

1   Preheat oven to 160ºC. Grease and flour a 24 cm spring-form cake tin.

2   Combine water, butter, chocolate and sugar together in a saucepan. Stir over a low heat until sugar has dissolved. Allow to cool to room temperature.

3   Sift together flour and cocoa and gently stir into chocolate mixture. Lightly whisk in beaten eggs and vanilla.

4   Pour into prepared cake tin. Bake for 1 hour or until a skewer inserted comes out clean. Allow to cool before removing from tin.

5   Once cold, ice with chocolate icing.

Sour chocolate icing:

1   Melt chocolate carefully. Stir in sour cream to form a smooth icing. Pour over cold cake and allow to set.

Serves 12

WHITE CHOCOLATE, COCONUT and PEACH FRIANDS

Fresh from the oven these little cakes give off a sweet almond aroma that is so totally seductive I can hardly keep myself from eating several immediately. They are only worth resisting because once on display in the café it gives me pleasure to watch customers reacting likewise.

100 g butter

100 g white chocolate melts

1 cup fine desiccated coconut

1½ cups icing sugar

½ cup plain flour

6 egg whites

1 tsp vanilla extract

2 fresh peaches (or drained canned peach slices)

1 Heat oven to 180ºC. Grease 10 oval or muffin pans.

2 Gently melt butter and white chocolate together. Place all ingredients except peaches into a mixing bowl. Stir until just combined. Pour mixture into prepared pans – they should be just over half full. Top each with a couple of peach slices. Bake for 25 minutes.

3 Allow to stand in pans for 5 minutes before turning out on to a cooling rack.

Makes 10

CRANBERRY and SEMOLINA RICOTTA CAKE

This continental-style curd cake has a rather startling consistency and elegant flavour.

ground almonds for dusting

150 g butter

1½ cups sugar

4 eggs, separated

600 g ricotta

finely grated zest and juice of 2 lemons

½ cup semolina

¾ cup ground almonds

½ cup dried cranberries (raisins also work well)

1 Preheat oven to 160ºC. Grease a 22 cm spring-form cake tin and dust with ground almonds.

2 Cream butter and sugar until pale. Beat in egg yolks, ricotta, zest and juice. Fold in semolina, ground almonds and cranberries and mix well.

3 Whisk egg whites to soft peaks and gently fold into cake mixture. Pour into prepared cake tin. Bake for 45 minutes or until a skewer inserted comes out clean.

Serves 10

SO TOTALLY SEDUCTIVE I CAN HARDLY
KEEP MYSELF FROM EATING SEVERAL

White Chocolate, Coconut and Peach Friands

INDEX